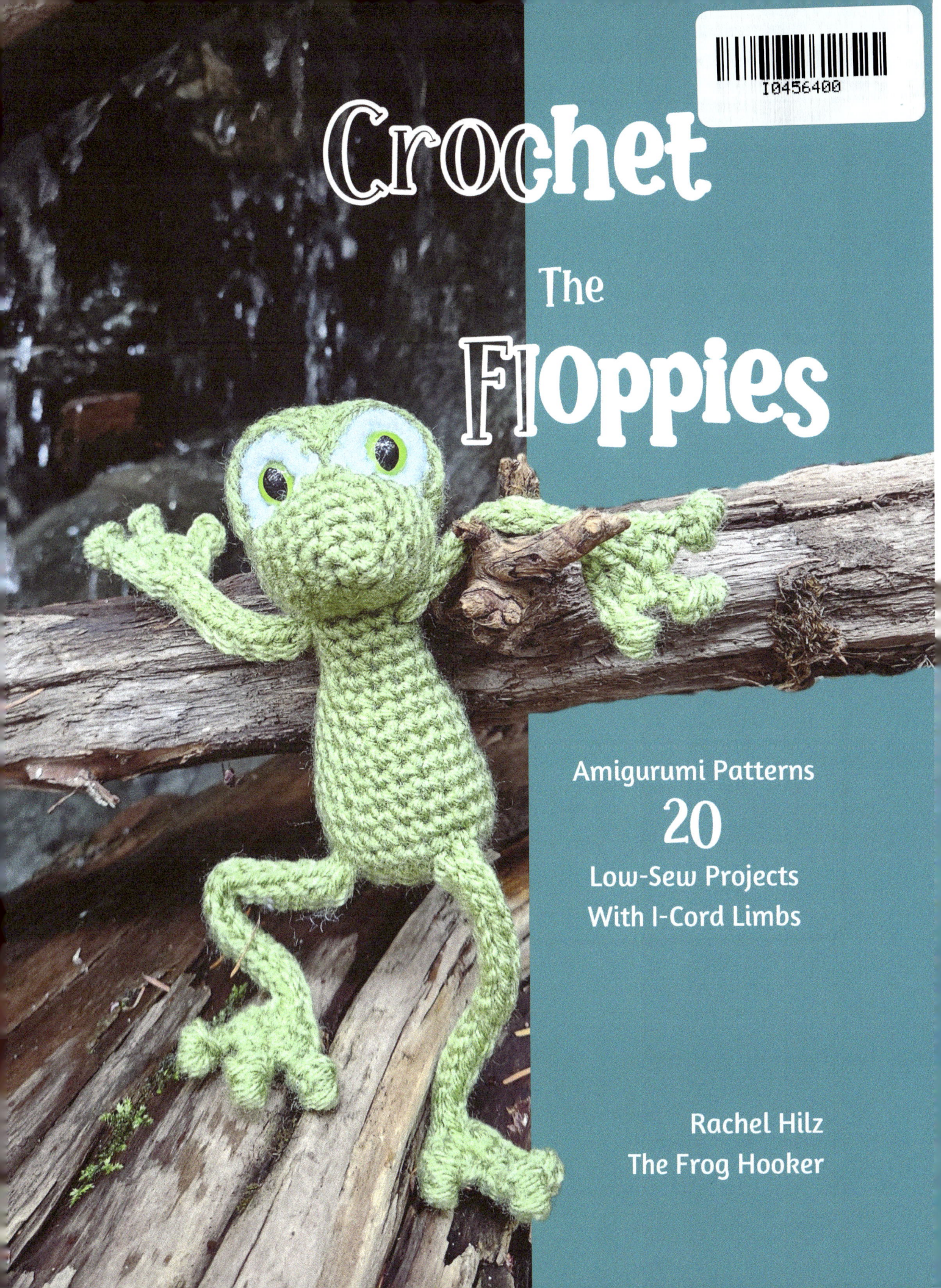

Crochet

The
Floppies

Amigurumi Patterns
20
Low-Sew Projects
With I-Cord Limbs

Rachel Hilz
The Frog Hooker

To my incredible husband who handled the daily circus of parenting while I turned yarn into critters. Your kid and dog-wrangling skills are unmatched. This book is as much yours as it is mine! Thanks for keeping the ice-caps flowing and the chaos contained.

Special Thanks to my Pattern Testers:
Aimee J Borst - Manic Yarn
Brenda Cooper - B's Happy Hookery
Cathy Robinson - Stitch Witchery
Georgie Aragon
JoAnna Weber
Nikki King - Nikki Nacky Needles
Shay Sharon Stanton
Tina Marie Doucet-Haughie
and to my Editor, Bobbie Hinman
This book could not have happened without your help and support.

ISBN: 978-1-990531-45-3 (hardcover) | 978-1-990531-46-0 (paperback) | 978-1-990531-47-7 (Kindle) | 978-1-990531-48-4 (spiral bound)

General info for all patterns in this book

All the Floppies use the same base pattern, with changes introduced as we progress in complexity.

We begin with the Chihuahua pattern which uses basic amigurumi stitches and techniques (with the exception of the I-cord limbs) and finish the book with Floppy Lion, who sports a wig cap made with Double Loop stitches.

This book is designed for people who would like to explore and play with multiple stitches and techniques. Amigurumi doesn't have to be only single crochet stitches. We can experiment and have fun.

The Floppy patterns are written using US terminology.

YARN

I have used Super Saver yarn by Red Heart for all the patterns in this book. It is a worsted weight yarn, or a medium 4. The Floppies don't use much, so they are great for scrap busting.

Although the Floppies in this book are shown in worsted weight, half the fun of amigurumi is experimenting with different yarns. So, go ahead and have fun with it. Remember to use a hook at least one to two sizes smaller than recommended on the skein. This will give you the tight stitches wanted in amigurumi.

HOOK SIZE

A size 4 mm hook is used throughout this book.

This is the largest hook size I advise for most amigurumi. There are exceptions to this, such as in areas without stuffing or where the crocheted fabric is double-layered. I like a size 4 because it is easier on my hands than smaller hooks, but it still creates a tight enough stitch.

Feel free to use the hook you are most comfortable with. Please keep in mind that any changes to the hook size will affect the size of the completed toy.

GAUGE

Gauge is not important for these patterns. Just be sure it's tight so your fiberfill doesn't show through your stitches. If your stitches tend to be loose, you might want to go down an additional hook size to compensate for this.

SIZE

Most Floppies measure 9" to 10" in length from head to toe when made with the recommended yarn and hook. This varies when ears are added. Some animals have longer legs, which add a bit of length, and some (like Duck and Tortoise) have shorter legs.

3

Contents

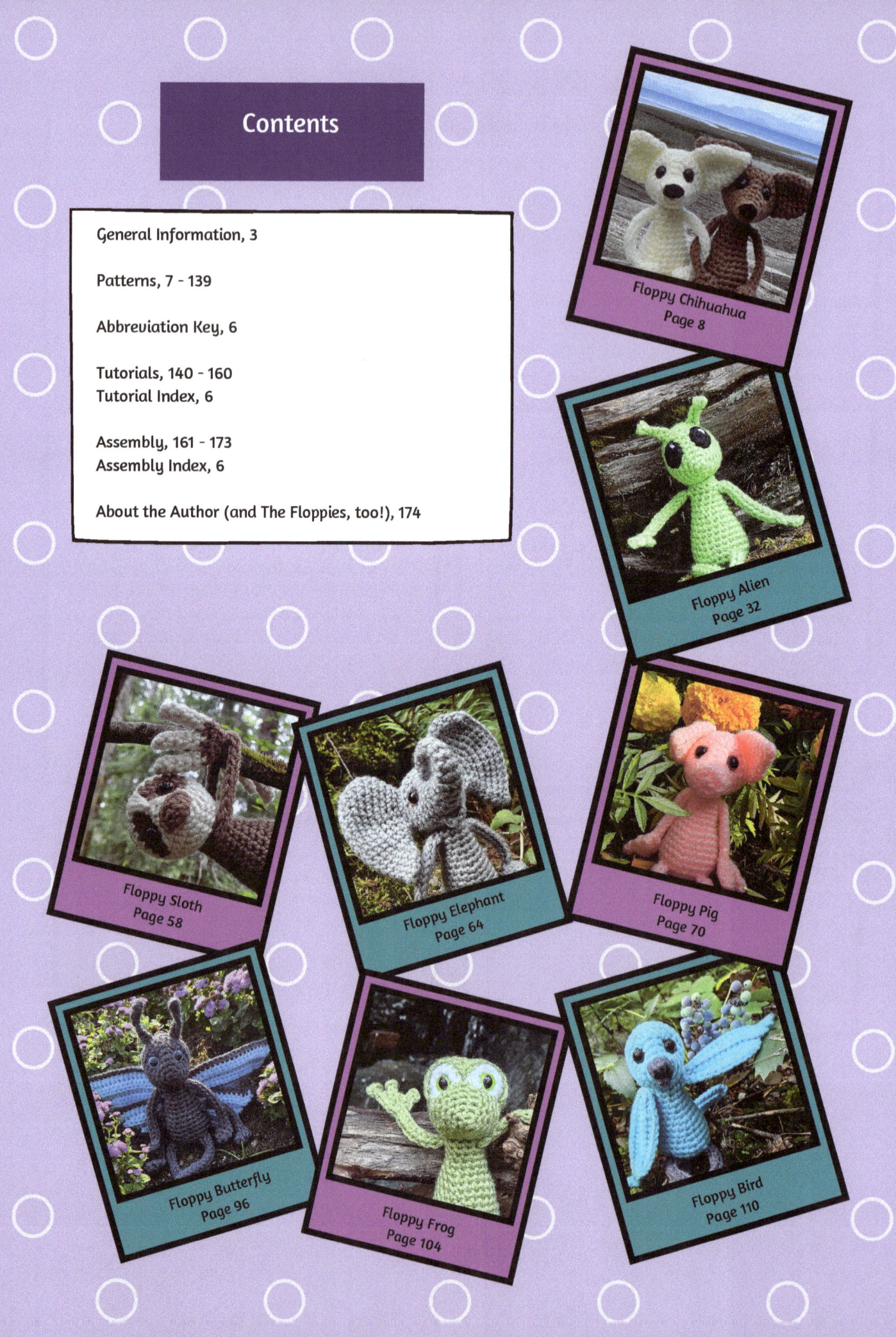

Floppy Chihuahua
Page 8

Floppy Alien
Page 32

Floppy Sloth
Page 58

Floppy Elephant
Page 64

Floppy Pig
Page 70

Floppy Butterfly
Page 96

Floppy Frog
Page 104

Floppy Bird
Page 110

Tutorial Index

Assembly Index

Abbreviation key

BLO - Back Loop Only

Cc - Color Change

Ch - Chain

Dc - Double Crochet

Dc2tog - Double Crochet Two Together

Dlst - Double Loop Stitch

Ea - Each

FLO - Front Loop Only

FO - Finish Off

Fpdc - Front Post Double Crochet

Hdc - Half Double Crochet

Inc - Increase

PM - Place Marker

Sc - Single Crochet

Sc2tog - Single Crochet Two Together

Sc3tog - Single Crochet Three Together

Sk - Skip

Sl st - Slip Stitch

Slst2tog - Slip stitch Two Together

St(s)- Stitch or Stitches

Tr - Treble

Yo - Yarn Over

Floppy Chihuahua

MATERIALS:

- Worsted weight yarn (medium 4)
  - Red Heart Super Saver in Cafe Latte (32.5 g for Long-nosed Chihuahua)
  - Red Heart Super Saver in Soft White (32.5 g for Short-nosed Chihuahua)
  - Red Heart Super Saver in Black for nose (about a 30" length)
- 4 mm hook
- Stitch marker(s)
- Scissors
- Fiberfill
- 12 mm safety eyes in brown
- Doll-making needle
- Optional: one 3/32" x 1 ½" cotter pin, one 3/32" x 3/16" hitch pin clip, two 3/16" fender washers, two No. 6 countersunk finishing washers, and pliers for bending the cotter pin (if you are doing the jointed neck)

ABBREVIATIONS USED IN THIS FLOPPY:

Ea - Each
FLO - Front Loop Only
FO - Finish Off
Hdc - Half Double Crochet
Inc - Increase

PM - Place Marker
Sc - Single Crochet
Sc2tog - Single Crochet Two Together
St(s) - Stitch or Stitches
Yo - Yarn Over

Floppy Chihuahua Teaches:

- Reading a Pattern - pg. 141
- Basic Stitches - see Tutorial Index - pg. 6
- I-cord - pgs. 142 & 143
- Magic ring - pg. 145
- Needle sculpting - pg. 166
- Cotter pin Neck Joint (optional) - pg. 169
- Assembly - See Assembly Index - pg. 6

9

EARS (Make 2)

- Working top to bottom
- Working in continuous rounds
- Working with main color

Round 1: 5 sc in a magic ring (5)
Round 2: (sc in ea st) around (5)
Round 3: (sc inc in ea st) around (10)
Round 4: (sc in ea st) around (10)
Round 5: (sc in the next st, sc inc) around (15)
Round 6: (sc in ea st) around (15)
Round 7: (sc in the next 2 sts, sc inc) around (20)
Round 8: (sc2tog, sc in the next 2 sts) around (15)
Round 9: sc2tog, sc 13 (14)

- FO.
- Do not stuff.
- Set aside until Round 10 of the head for short-nosed chihuahua.
- Set aside until Round 12 of the head for long-nosed chihuahua.

NOSE

- Working with Dark Charcoal yarn.
- Starting and finishing with long tail to use when sewing in place.

Row 1: sc 3 into magic ring - Pull to close but do not join.

- FO.
- Set aside until the head is complete.
- Sew in place with the bottom point of the nose at the center of the magic ring that was used to start the head.

HEAD FOR LONG-NOSED (DEER HEAD) CHIHUAHUA

- Working from the nose to the back of the head
- Working in continuous rounds
- Working with main color

Round 1: sc 4 in a magic ring (4)
Round 2: (sc inc in each st) around (8)
Round 3 - Round 4: (sc in ea st) around (8)
Round 5: (sc in the next st, sc inc) around (12)
Round 6: (sc in ea st) around (12)
Round 7: (sc in the next 2 sts, sc inc) around (16)
Round 8: (sc in the next 3 sts, sc inc) around (20)
Round 9: (sc in the next 4 sts, sc inc) around (24)
Round 10: sc in the next 3 sts, (1 hdc, hdc inc) three times, 1 hdc, sc in the next 7 sts, (sc2tog) two times, sc in remaining 3 sts (25)
- PM in base of 1st and last hdc sts of Round 10
Round 11: (sc in ea st) around (25)
Round 12: sc 7 while joining ear, sc 3, sc 7 while joining ear, sc 8 (25)
Round 13: (sc in ea st) around (25)
Round 14: (sc in the next 3 sts, sc2tog) around (20)
Round 15: (sc in the next 2 sts, sc2tog) around (15)
Round 16: (sc in the next st, sc2tog) around (10)

- FO with a long tail.
- Place eyes at the base of the 1st and last hdc sts (where you placed your stitch markers).
- Place cotter pin (if jointing the neck) at bottom/center between Round 10 & Round 11.
- Stuff the head.
- Use the long end for the drawstring close and for needle sculpting to tuck the eyes, if desired.
- Sew on the nose.
- Set the head aside until Round 4 of the body (if jointing the neck) or until the body is completed (if sewing the head in place).

HEAD FOR SHORT-NOSED (APPLE HEAD) CHIHUAHUA

- Working from the nose to the back of the head
- Working in continuous rounds
- Working with main color

Round 1: sc 6 in a magic ring (6)
Round 2: (sc inc in each st) around (12)
Round 3 - Round 4: (sc in ea st) around (12)
Round 5: (FLO sc in the next 2 sts, FLO sc inc) around (16)
Round 6: (sc in the next 3 sts, sc inc) around (20)
Round 7: (sc in the next 4 sts, sc inc) around (24)
Round 8: sc in the next 3 sts, (1 hdc, hdc inc) three times, 1 hdc, sc in the next 7 sts, (sc2tog) two times, sc in remaining 3 sts (25)
  - PM in base of 1st and last hdc sts of Round 8
Round 9: (sc in ea st) around (25)
Round 10: sc 7 while joining ear, sc 3, sc 7 while joining ear, sc 8 (25)
Round 11: (sc in ea st) around (25)
Round 12: (sc in the next 3 sts, sc2tog) around (20)
Round 13: (sc in the next 2 sts, sc2tog) around (15)
Round 14: (sc in the next st, sc2tog) around (10)

- FO with a long tail.
- Place eyes at the base of the 1st and last hdc sts (where you placed your stitch markers).
- Place cotter pin (if jointing the neck) at bottom/center between Round 8 & Round 9.
- Stuff the head.
- Use the long end for the drawstring close and for needle sculpting to tuck the eyes, if desired.
- Sew on the nose.
- Set the head aside until Round 4 of the body (if jointing the neck) or until the body is completed (if sewing the head in place).

HANDS and ARMS (Make 2)

- Working in continuous rounds
- Starting with the hand and working into the arm
- Working with main color

Round 1: 6 sc in a magic ring (6)
Round 2 - Round 3: (sc in ea st) around (6)

- Tuck the end into the hand.
- Do not stuff.
- Pull up two more loops evenly spaced across the opening of hand; this closes the hand and provides the loops needed to start the I-cord (3 loops on hook).

I-CORD ARMS

- Working in rows
- Do NOT turn

Row 1: Drop 2 loops (pinching them so they don't unravel), ch 1, pick up 2nd loop & ch 1, pick up last loop & ch 1
Row 2 - Row 12: repeat Row 1

- To finish, yo, pull through all three, cut yarn, yo, pull through one.
- Set aside until Round 3 of the body

FEET and LEGS (Make 2)

- Working in continuous rounds
- Starting with the foot and working into the leg
- Working with main color

Round 1: 6 sc in a magic ring (6)
Round 2: (sc inc in ea st) around (12)
Round 3: (sc in ea st) around (12)
Round 4: (sc2tog) six times (6)

- Tuck the end into the foot.
- Do not stuff.
- Pull up two more loops evenly spaced across the opening of the foot; this closes the foot and provides the loops needed to start the I-cord (3 loops on hook).

I-CORD LEGS

- Working in rows
- Do NOT turn

Row 1: Drop 2 loops (pinching them so they don't unravel), ch 1, pick up 2nd loop & ch 1, pick up last loop & ch 1
Row 2 - Row 17: repeat Row 1

- To finish, yo, pull through all three, cut yarn, yo, pull through one.
- Set aside until Round 15 of the body.

TAIL

- Working from tip to base
- Working in continuous rounds
- Working with main color

Round 1: sc 4 in a magic ring (4)
Round 2 - Round 3: (sc in ea st) around (4)
Round 4: (sc in next st, sc inc) around (6)
Round 5 - Round 13: (sc in ea st) around (6)

- FO.
- Do not stuff.
- Set aside until Round 15 of the body.

BODY

- Working from the neck down
- Working in continuous rounds
- Working with main color

Round 1: sc 6 in a magic ring (6)
Round 2: (sc inc) around (12)
Round 3: sc 3, sc 2 while joining 1st arm, sc 4, sc 2 while joining 2nd arm, sc 1 (12)
Round 4: (sc in ea st) around (12)
- Install cotter pin if jointing the neck
Round 5: (sc in ea st) around (12)
Round 6: (sc in the next 3 sts, sc inc) around (15)
Round 7: (sc in ea st) around (15)
Round 8: (sc in the next 4 sts, sc inc) around (18)
Round 9: (sc in the next 5 sts, sc inc) around (21)
Round 10 - Round 11: (sc in ea st) around (21)
Round 12: (sc in the next 6 sts, sc inc) around (24)
Round 13: (sc in the next 7 sts, sc inc) around (27)
Round 14: (sc in ea st) around (27)
Round 15: sc 3, sc 3 while joining tail, sc 8, sc 2 while joining 1st leg, sc 5, sc 2 while joining 2nd leg, sc 4 (27)
Round 16: (sc in the next st, sc2tog) around (18)
- Stuff the body
Round 17: repeat round 16 (12)
Round 18: (sc2tog) around (6)

- FO & drawstring close.
- Sew the head to the body if you didn't joint the neck.

Floppy Teddy Bear

MATERIALS:

- Worsted weight yarn (medium 4)
  - Red Heart Super Saver in Light Blue (26 g)
  - Red Heart Super Saver in Soft White (1.5 g)
  - Red Heart Super Saver in Black for nose (about a 40" length)
- 4 mm hook
- Stitch marker(s)
- Scissors
- Fiberfill
- 12 mm safety eyes in blue
- Doll-making needle
- Optional: one 3/32" x 1 ½" cotter pin, one 3/32" x 3/16" hitch pin clip, two 3/16" fender washers, two No. 6 countersunk finishing washers, and pliers for bending the cotter pin (if you are doing the jointed neck)

ABBREVIATIONS USED IN THIS FLOPPY:

Ea - Each

FLO - Front Loop Only

FO - Finish Off

Hdc - Half Double Crochet

Inc - Increase

PM - Place Marker

Sc - Single Crochet

Sc2tog - Single Crochet Two Together

Sl st - Slip Stitch

St(s) - Stitch or Stitches

YO - Yarn Over

Floppy Teddy Bear Teaches:

- Slip Stitch - pg. 156
- Joining with a Single Crochet Stitch - pg. 154
- Front Loop only - pg. 147

EARS (Make 2)

- Working from top to base
- Working in continuous rounds
- Working with main color

Round 1: sc 6 in a magic ring(6)
Round 2: (sc inc in ea st) around (12)
Round 3: (sc into ea st) around (12)

- FO.
- Do not stuff.
- Set aside until Round 10 of the head.

NOSE

- Working with Black yarn.
- Start and finish with long tail to use when sewing in place.

Row 1: sc 3 into magic ring, pull to close but do not join.

- FO.
- Set aside until the head is complete.
- Sew in place with the bottom point of the nose at the center of the magic ring that was used to start the head.
- Make the mouth with the starting yarn of the nose.

HEAD

- Working from the nose to the back of the head
- Working in continuous rounds
- Starting in the lighter color for the muzzle (Soft White)

Round 1: sc 6 in a magic ring(6)
Round 2: (sc inc in ea st) around (12)
Round 3 - Round 4: (sc in ea st) around (12)

- Sl st in next st and FO
- Change to main color

Round 5: (in FLO sc in the next 2 sts, FLO sc inc) around (16)
Round 6: (sc in the next 3 sts, sc inc) around (20)
Round 7: (sc in the next 4 sts, sc inc) around (24)
Round 8: sc in the next 3 sts, (1 hdc, hdc inc) three times, 1 hdc, sc in the next 7 sts, (sc2tog) two times, sc in remaining 3 sts (25)

- PM in base of 1st and last hdc sts of Round 8

Round 9: (sc in ea st) around (25)
Round 10: sc 1, sc 6 while joining ear, sc 3, sc 6 while joining ear, sc 9 (25)
Round 11: (sc in ea st) around (25)
Round 12: (sc in the next 3 sts, sc2tog) around (20)
Round 13: (sc in the next 2 sts, sc2tog) around (15)
Round 14: (sc in the next st, sc2tog) around (10)

- FO with a long tail.
- Place eyes at the base of the 1st and last hdc sts (where you placed your stitch markers).
- Place cotter pin (if jointing the neck) at bottom/center between Round 8 & Round 9.
- Stuff the head.
- Use the long end for the drawstring close and for needle sculpting to tuck the eyes, if desired.
- Sew on the nose.
- Set the head aside until Round 4 of the body (if jointing the neck) or until the body is completed (if sewing the head in place).

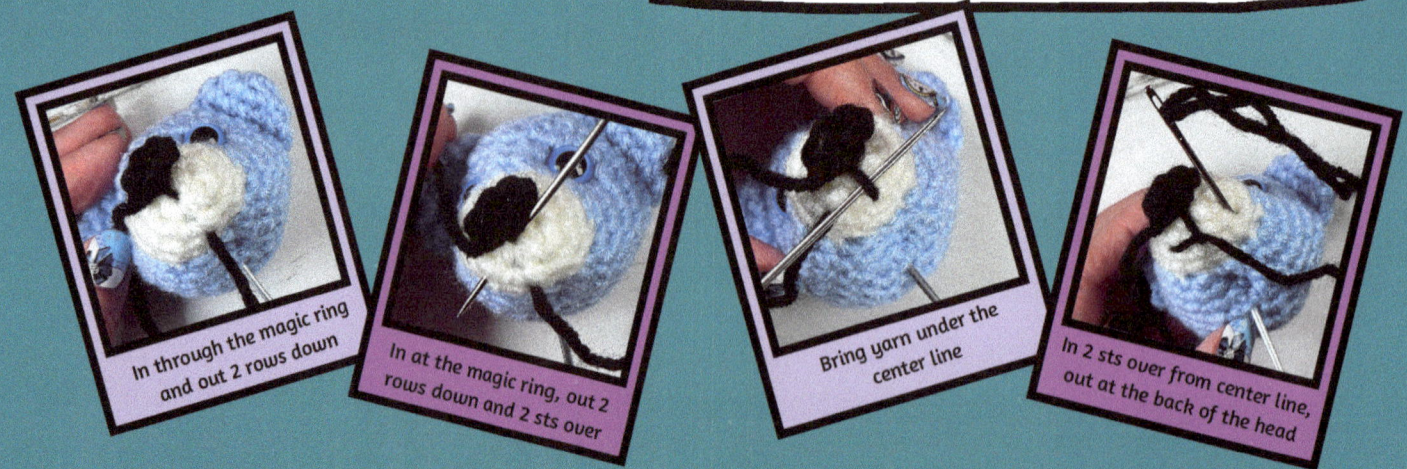

In through the magic ring and out 2 rows down

In at the magic ring, out 2 rows down and 2 sts over

Bring yarn under the center line

In 2 sts over from center line, out at the back of the head

HANDS and ARMS (Make 2)

- Working in continuous rounds
- Starting with the hand and working into the arm
- Working with main color

Round 1: 6 sc in a magic ring (6)
Round 2 - Round 3: (sc in ea st) around (6)

- Tuck the end into the hand.
- Do not stuff.
- Pull up two more loops evenly spaced across the opening of the hand; this closes the hand and provides the loops needed to start the I-cord (3 loops on hook).

I-CORD ARMS

- Working in rows
- Do NOT turn

Row 1: Drop 2 loops (pinching them so they don't unravel), ch 1, pick up 2nd loop & ch 1, pick up last loop & ch 1
Row 2 - Row 12: repeat Row 1

- To finish, yo, pull through all three, cut yarn, yo, pull through one.
- Set aside until Round 3 of the body.

FEET and LEGS (Make 2)

- Working in continuous rounds
- Starting with the foot and working into the leg
- Working with main color

Round 1: 6 sc in a magic ring (6)
Round 2: (sc inc in ea st) around (12)
Round 3: (sc in ea st) around (12)
Round 4: (sc2tog) six times (6)

- Tuck the end into the foot.
- Do not stuff.
- Pull up two more loops evenly spaced across the opening of the foot; this closes the foot and provides the loops needed to start the I-cord (3 loops on hook).

I-CORD LEGS

- Working in rows
- Do NOT turn

Row 1: Drop 2 loops (pinching them so they don't unravel), ch 1, pick up 2nd loop & ch 1, pick up last loop & ch 1
Row 2 - Row 17: repeat Row 1

- To finish, yo, pull through all three, cut yarn, yo, pull through one.
- Set aside until Round 15 of the body.

Red Heart, Super Saver in Baby Pink

BODY

- Working from the neck down
- Working in continuous rounds
- Working with main color

Round 1: sc 6 in a magic ring (6)
Round 2: (sc inc) around (12)
Round 3: sc 3, sc 2 while joining 1st arm, sc 4, sc 2 while joining 2nd arm, sc 1 (12)
Round 4: (sc in ea st) around (12)
- Install cotter pin if jointing the neck
Round 5: (sc in ea st) around (12)
Round 6: (sc in the next 3 sts, sc inc) around (15)
Round 7: (sc in ea st) around (15)
Round 8: (sc in the next 4 sts, sc inc) around (18)
Round 9: (sc in the next 5 sts, sc inc) around (21)
Round 10 - Round 11: (sc in ea st) around (21)
Round 12: (sc in the next 6 sts, sc inc) around (24)
Round 13: (sc in the next 7 sts, sc inc) around (27)
Round 14: (sc in ea st) around (27)
Round 15: sc 3, sc 2 while joining tail, sc 8, sc 2 while joining 1st leg, sc 5, sc 2 while joining 2nd leg, sc 5 (27)
Round 16: (sc in the next st, sc2tog) around (18)
- Stuff the body
Round 17: repeat round 16 (12)
Round 18: (sc2tog) around (6)

- FO & drawstring close.
- Sew the head to the body if you didn't joint the neck.

TAIL

- Working with main color

Row 1: sc, 6 hdc, sc in a magic ring (8)

- Pull magic circle closed but do not join.
- FO.
- Set aside until Round 15 of the body.

Red Heart, Super Saver in Oatmeal

Floppy Mouse

MATERIALS:

- Worsted weight yarn (medium 4)
  - Red Heart Super Saver in Soapstone (28 g)
  - Red Heart Super Saver in Baby Pink for nose (about a 30" length)
- 4 mm hook
- Stitch marker(s)
- Scissors
- Fiberfill
- 12 mm safety eyes in brown
- Doll-making needle
- Dental floss for whiskers
- Optional: one 3/32" x 1 ½" cotter pin, one 3/32" x 3/16" hitch pin clip, two 3/16" fender washers, two No. 6 countersunk finishing washers, and pliers for bending the cotter pin (if you are doing the jointed neck)

ABBREVIATIONS USED IN THIS FLOPPY:

Ch - Chain
Ea - Each
FO - Finish Off
Hdc - Half Double Crochet
Inc - Increase
PM - Place Marker

Sc - Single Crochet
Sc2tog - Single Crochet Two Together
Sk - Skip
Sl st - Slip Stitch
St(s) - Stitch or Stitches
Yo - Yarn Over

Floppy Mouse Teaches:

- How to add whiskers – pg. 22
- Working in rows – pg. 157
- Chain Stitch – pg. 144
- Rooting – pg. 173
- Back Bump of the Chain – pg. 144

21

EARS (Make 2)

- Working from top to base
- Working in continuous rounds

Round 1: sc 6 in a magic ring (6)
Round 2: (sc inc in ea st) around (12)
Round 3: (sc into ea st) around (12)
Round 4: (sc in the next st, sc inc) around (18)
Round 5: sc2tog, sc 7, sc2tog, sc 7 (16)
Round 6: (sc2tog) around (8)

- FO.
- Do not stuff.
- Set aside until Round 9 of the head.

NOSE

- Working with Pink yarn (Baby Pink)
- Starting and finishing with long tail to use when sewing in place

Row 1: sc 3 into magic ring, pull to close but do not join

- FO.
- Set aside until the head is complete.
- Sew in place with the bottom point of the nose at the center of the magic ring that was used to start the head.

HEAD

- Working from the nose to the back of the head
- Working in continuous rounds

Round 1: sc 4 in a magic ring (4)
Round 2: (sc inc each st) around (8)
Round 3: (sc in the next st, sc inc) around (12)
Round 4: (sc in the next 2 sts, sc inc) around (16)
Round 5: (sc in the next 3 sts, sc inc) around (20)
Round 6: (sc in the next 4 sts, sc inc) around (24)
Round 7: sc in the next 3 sts, (1 hdc, hdc inc) three times, 1 hdc, sc in the next 7 sts, (sc2tog) two times, sc in remaining 3 sts (25)
  - PM in base of 1st and last hdc sts of Round 7
Round 8: (sc in ea st) around (25)
Round 9: sc 3, sc 4 while attaching ear, sc 4, sc 4 while attaching the 2nd ear, sc 10 (25)
Round 10: (sc in ea st) around (25)
Round 11: (sc in the next 3 sts, sc2tog) around (20)
Round 12: (sc in the next 2 sts, sc2tog) around (15)
Round 13: (sc in the next st, sc2tog) around (10)

- FO with a long tail.
- Place eyes at the base of the 1st and last hdc sts (where you placed your stitch markers).
- Place cotter pin (if jointing the neck) at bottom/center between Round 7 & Round 8.
- Stuff the head.
- Use the long end for the drawstring close and for needle sculpting to tuck the eyes, if desired.
- Sew on the nose.
- Set the head aside until Round 4 of the body (if jointing the neck) or until the body is completed (if sewing the head in place).
- Add whiskers as pictured below.

Tie 4 strands of dental floss together, bring 2 under nose

Bring the other 2 stands under the nose 1 stitch down

Double knot the ends together

Cut to desired length

ARMS and HANDS (Make 2)

- Starting with the I-cord arm and working into the hand
- Do NOT turn while working the I-cord
- Note: There is a left and right hand; make one of each

Row 1: ch 3
Row 2: Insert hook in 2nd ch from hook, yo, pull up loop, insert hook in 3rd ch from hook, yo, pull up loop (3 loops on hook)
Row 3: Drop 2 loops (pinching them so they don't unravel), ch 1, pick up 2nd loop & ch 1, pick up last loop & ch 1
Row 4 - Row 12: repeat Row 3

- Do not FO.
- Start on appropriate hand.

RIGHT HAND

Row 13: yo, pull through all three (1 loop on hook), ch 2, sc 2 in the back bump of the 2nd ch from hook (wrist formed)
Row 14: ch 2, turn, sk 2 ch sts, sl st into 1st sc (thumb formed), ch 2, 1 hdc into the same st as sl st, hdc in next sc st
Row 15: turn, but do not ch 1, sk 1st hdc, sl st in the top of the next hdc

- FO.
- Darn the loose end into the hand.
- Set aside until Round 3 of the body.

LEFT HAND

Row 13: yo, pull through all three (1 loop on hook), ch 3, sl st in back bump of 2nd ch from hook (thumb formed), sc 2 in the back bump of the remaining ch (wrist formed)
Row 14: ch 2, turn, hdc 1 in ea of the 2 sc sts
Row 15: turn, but do not ch 1, sk 1st hdc, sl st in the top of the next hdc

- FO.
- Darn the loose end into the hand.
- Set aside until Round 3 of the body.

FEET and LEGS (Make 2)

- Working in continuous rounds
- Starting with the foot and working into the leg

Round 1: 6 sc in a magic ring (6)
Round 2: (sc inc in ea st) around (12)
Round 3: (sc in ea st) around (12)
Round 4: (sc2tog) six times (6)

- Tuck the end into the foot.
- Do not stuff.
- Pull up two more loops evenly spaced across the opening of the foot; this closes the foot and provides the loops needed to start the I-cord (3 loops on hook).

I-CORD LEGS

- Working in rows
- Do NOT turn

Row 1: Drop 2 loops (pinching them so they don't unravel), ch 1, pick up 2nd loop & ch 1, pick up last loop & ch 1
Row 2 - Row 17: repeat Row 1

- To finish, yo, pull through all three, cut yarn, yo, pull through one.
- Set aside until Round 15 of the body.

BODY

- Working from the neck down
- Working in continuous rounds

Round 1: sc 6 in a magic ring (6)
Round 2: (sc inc) around (12)
Round 3: sc 3, sc 3 while joining right arm, sc 3, sc 3 while joining left arm (12)
- Double check your arms are placed correctly, with thumbs facing forward (your stitch marker in on his back)
Round 4: (sc in ea st) around (12)
- Install cotter pin if jointing the neck
Round 5: (sc in ea st) around (12)
Round 6: (sc in the next 3 sts, sc inc) around (15)
Round 7: (sc in ea st) around (15)
Round 8: (sc in the next 4 sts, sc inc) around (18)
Round 9: (sc in the next 5 sts, sc inc) around (21)
Round 10 - Round 11: (sc in ea st) around (21)
Round 12: (sc in the next 6 sts, sc inc) around (24)
Round 13: (sc in the next 7 sts, sc inc) around (27)
Round 14: (sc in ea st) around (27)
Round 15: sc 14, sc 2 while joining 1st leg, sc 5, sc 2 while joining 2nd leg, sc 4 (27)
Round 16: (sc in the next st, sc2tog) around (18)
- Stuff the body
Round 17: repeat round 16 (12)
Round 18: (sc2tog) around (6)

- FO & drawstring close.
- Sew the head to the body if you didn't joint the neck.

TAIL

- Starting and finishing with a long tail for sewing.
- Attach to the bum with a sc at the back/center of Round 15.

Row 1: ch 18

- FO with a long tail (about 15" long).
- Sew through ea st up the tail (going through the same side of the back bump of ch ea time).
- Hide the ends in the body.

Floppy Ladybug

MATERIALS:

- Worsted weight yarn (medium 4)
  - Red Heart Super Saver in Charcoal (25 g)
  - Red Heart Super Saver in Hot Red (11.5 g)
  - Red Heart Super Saver in Black (3 g)
- 4 mm hook
- Stitch marker(s)
- Scissors
- Fiberfill
- 12 mm safety eyes in blue
- Doll-making needle
- Optional: one 3/32" x 1 ½" cotter pin, one 3/32" x 3/16" hitch pin clip, two 3/16" fender washers, two No. 6 countersunk finishing washers, and pliers for bending the cotter pin (if you are doing the jointed neck)

ABBREVIATIONS USED IN THIS FLOPPY:

St(s) - Stitch or Stitches

FO - Finish Off

Ea - Each

Inc - Increase

PM - Place Marker

Sc - Single Crochet

Sc2tog - Single Crochet Two Together

Hdc - Half Double Crochet

Ch - Chain

Yo - Yarn Over

Sl st - Slip Stitch

Floppy Ladybug Teaches:

- Puff Stitch Antennae - pg. 159
- Working around the chain - pg. 159
- Joining the Antennae - pg. 168

27

ANTENNA (Make 2)

Special Stitch Instructions for Puff Stitch: Yo, insert in back bump of the 2nd ch from hook, yo, pull up loop, yo, insert hook into same st, yo, pull up loop, yo, pull through all 5 loops on the hook.

- Working with Dark Grey yarn (Charcoal).
- Start and finish with a long tail for tying off inside head.

Row 1: ch 7
Row 2: puff st in 2nd ch from the hook, sl st in the same st, sc 6 AROUND the ch, sc in the back bump of the last ch st.

- FO.
- Set aside until Round 8 of the head.

HEAD

- Working from the nose to the back of the head
- Working in continuous rounds
- Working with Dark Grey yarn (Charcoal)

Round 1: sc 6 into a magic ring (6)
Round 2: (sc inc in ea st) around (12)
Round 3: (sc in the next 2 sts, sc inc) around (16)
Round 4: (sc in the next 3 sts, sc inc) around (20)
Round 5: (sc in the next 4 sts, sc inc) around (24)
Round 6: sc in the next 3 sts, (1 hdc, 2 hdc) three times, 1 hdc, sc in the next 7 sts, (sc2tog) two times, sc in remaining 3 sts (25)
- PM in base of 1st and last hdc sts of Round 6

Round 7: (sc in ea st) around (25)
Round 8: sc 6, sc 1 while attaching antenna, sc 3, sc 1 while attaching the 2nd antenna, sc 14 (25)
- Make sure the antennae are placed so they curve toward the outer sides of the head.

Round 9: (sc in ea st) around (25)
- Tie the ends of the antenna together inside of the head.

Round 10: (sc in the next 3 sts, sc2tog) around (20)
Round 11: (sc in the next 2 sts, sc2tog) around (15)
Round 12: (sc in the next st, sc2tog) around (10)

- FO with a long tail.
- Place eyes at the base of the 1st and last hdc sts (where you placed your stitch markers).
- Place cotter pin (if jointing the neck) at bottom/center between Round 8 & Round 9.
- Stuff the head.
- Use the long end for the drawstring close and for needle sculpting to tuck the eyes, if desired.
- Set head aside until Round 4 of the body (if jointing the neck) or until the body is completed (if sewing the head in place).

HANDS and ARMS (Make 4)

- Working in continuous rounds
- Starting with the hand and working into the arm
- Working with Dark Grey yarn (Charcoal)

Round 1: 6 sc in a magic ring (6)
Round 2 - Round 3: (sc in ea st) around (6)

- Tuck the end into the hand.
- Do not stuff.
- Pull up two more loops evenly spaced across the opening of the hand; this closes the hand and provides the loops needed to start the I-cord (3 loops on hook).

I-CORD ARMS

- Working in rows
- Do NOT turn

Row 1: Drop 2 loops (pinching them so they don't unravel), ch 1, pick up 2nd loop & ch 1, pick up last loop & ch 1
Row 2 - Row 12: repeat Row 1

- To finish, yo, pull through all three, cut yarn, yo, pull through one.
- Set aside until Round 3 & Round 9 of the body.

FEET and LEGS (Make 2)

- Working in continuous rounds
- Starting with the foot and working into the leg
- Working with Dark Grey yarn (Charcoal)

Round 1: 6 sc in a magic ring (6)
Round 2: (sc inc in ea st) around (12)
Round 3: (sc in ea st) around (12)
Round 4: (sc2tog) six times (6)

- Tuck the end into the foot.
- Do not stuff.
- Pull up two more loops evenly spaced across the opening of the foot; this closes the foot and provides the loops needed to start the I-cord (3 loops on hook).

I-CORD LEGS

- Working in rows
- Do NOT turn

Row 1: Drop 2 loops (pinching them so they don't unravel), ch 1, pick up 2nd loop & ch 1, pick up last loop & ch 1
Row 2 - Row 17: repeat Row 1

- To finish, yo, pull through all three, cut yarn, yo, pull through one.
- Set aside until Round 15 of the body.

WINGS (Make 2)

- Working with Red yarn (Hot Red)
- Working in continuous rounds

Round 1: sc6 in magic ring (6)
Round 2: (sc inc) around (12)
Round 3: (sc in the next st, sc inc) around (18)
Round 4: (sc in the next 2 sts, sc inc) around (24)
Round 5: (sc in the next 3 sts, sc inc) around (30)
Round 6: (sc in the next 4 sts, sc inc) around (36)
Round 7 - Round 8: (sc in ea st) around (36)
Round 9: fold in half and sc the edges together with 18 sc sts (18)

- FO and set aside until Round 3 of the body.

BODY

- Working from the neck down
- Working in continuous rounds
- Working with Dark Grey yarn (Charcoal)

Round 1: sc 6 in a magic ring (6)
Round 2: (sc inc) around (12)
Round 3: sc 2 while joining 1st wing, sc 2 while joining 2nd wing, sc 2 while joining 1st arm, sc 4, sc 2 while joining 2nd arm (12)
- Double-check wing placement (The wing's magic circle should be in the center of the back, and the sc sts should be on the outer edges.)
Round 4: (sc in ea st) around (12)
- Install cotter pin if jointing the neck.
Round 5: (sc in ea st) around (12)
- Optional: tie the loose ends of the wings together inside the body for added security.
Round 6: (sc in the next 3 sts, sc inc) around (15)
Round 7: (sc in ea st) around (15)
Round 8: (sc in the next 4 sts, sc inc) around (18)
Round 9: sc 3, sc inc, sc 4, sc 2 while joining 3rd arm, sc, sc inc, sc 2, sc inc, sc, sc 2 while joining 4th arm (21)
Round 10 - Round 11: (sc in ea st) around (21)
Round 12: (sc in the next 6 sts, sc inc) around (24)
Round 13: (sc in the next 7 sts, sc inc) around (27)
Round 14: (sc in ea st) around (27)
Round 15: sc 15, sc 2 while joining 1st leg, sc 5, sc 2 while joining 2nd leg, sc 3 (27)
Round 16: (sc in the next st, sc2tog) around (18)
- Stuff the body
Round 17: repeat round 16 (12)
Round 18: (sc2tog) around (6)

- FO & drawstring close.
- Sew the head to the body if you didn't joint the neck.

Attaching wings- View from working side

Top view

SPOTS (Make 6)

- Working with Black yarn

Round 1: sc 6 in magic ring (6)

- Sl st in the 1st stitch.
- FO with long ends.
- Sew in place being careful to only sew through the top layer of the wings.

Floppy Alien

MATERIALS:

- Worsted weight yarn (medium 4)
  - Red Heart Super Saver in Spring Green (24 g)
  - Red Heart Super Saver in Black for eyes (2 g)
  - Red Heart Super Saver in White for the eye shine (about a 20" length)
- 4 mm hook
- Stitch marker(s)
- Scissors
- Fiberfill
- Doll-making needle
- Optional: one 3/32" x 1 ½" cotter pin, one 3/32" x 3/16" hitch pin clip, two 3/16" fender washers, two No. 6 countersunk finishing washers, and pliers for bending the cotter pin (if you are doing the jointed neck)

ABBREVIATIONS USED IN THIS FLOPPY:

Ch - Chain

Ea - Each

FO - Finish Off

Hdc - Half Double Crochet

Inc - Increase

Pm - Place Marker

Sc - Single Crochet

Sc2tog - Single Crochet Two Together

Sk - Skip

Sl st - Slip Stitch

St(s) - Stitch or Stitches

Yo - Yarn Over

Floppy Alien Teaches:

- Crochet eyes (Sewing Other Parts Together) - pg. 167

33

EYES (Make 2)

- Working with Black yarn
- Working into a magic circle

Round 1: sc 2, hdc 2, sc 2, hdc 2 into magic ring (8)

- Join with a sl st.
- FO.
- Set aside until the head is completed.

ANTENNA (Make 2)

Special Stitch Instructions for Puff Stitch:
Yo, insert in back bump of the 2nd ch from hook, yo, pull up loop, yo, insert hook into same st, yo, pull up loop, yo, pull through all 5 loops on the hook.

- Start and finish with a long tail for tying off inside the head.

Row 1: ch 4
Row 2: puff st in 2nd ch from the hook, sl st in the same st, sc 3 AROUND the ch, sc in the back bump of the last ch st.

- FO.
- Set aside until Round 9 of the head.

HEAD

- Working from the nose to the back of the head
- Working in continuous rounds

Round 1: sc 4 in a magic ring (4)
Round 2: (sc inc each st) around (8)
Round 3: (sc in the next st, sc inc) around (12)
Round 4: (sc in the next 2 sts, sc inc) around (16)
Round 5: (sc in the next 3 sts, sc inc) around (20)
Round 6: (sc in the next 4 sts, sc inc) around (24)
Round 7: sc in the next 3 sts, (1 hdc, hdc inc) three times, 1 hdc, sc in the next 7 sts, (sc2tog) two times, sc in remaining 3 sts (25)
- PM in base of 1st and last hdc sts of Round 7
Round 8: (sc in ea st) around (25)
Round 9: sc 6, sc 1 while attaching antenna, sc 3, sc 1 while attaching the 2nd antenna, sc 14 (25)
- Make sure the antennae are placed so they curve toward the outer sides of the head.
Round 10: (sc in ea st) around (25)
- Tie the ends of the antenna together inside of the head.
Round 11: (sc in the next 3 sts, sc2tog) around (20)
Round 12: (sc in the next 2 sts, sc2tog) around (15)
Round 13: (sc in the next st, sc2tog) around (10)

- FO with a long tail.
- Place cotter pin (if jointing the neck) at bottom/center between Round 7 & Round 8.
- Stuff the head.
- Use the long end for the drawstring close and for needle sculpting to tuck the eye areas over the 1st and last hdc sts, if desired.
- Sew the eyes in place over the 1st and last hdc sts (where you placed your stitch markers) & use White yarn to add eye shine.
- Set the head aside until Round 4 of the body (if jointing the neck) or until the body is completed (if sewing the head in place).

ARMS and HANDS (Make 2)

- Staring with the I-cord arm and working into the hand.
- Do NOT turn while working the I-cord.
- Note: There is a left and right hand; make one of each.

Row 1: ch 3
Row 2: insert hook in 2nd ch from hook, yo, pull up loop, insert hook in 3rd ch from hook, yo, pull up loop (3 loops on hook)
Row 3: Drop 2 loops (pinching them so they don't unravel), ch 1, pick up 2nd loop & ch 1, pick up last loop & ch 1
Row 4 - Row 12: repeat Row 3

- Do not FO.
- Start on appropriate hand.

RIGHT HAND

Row 13: yo, pull through all three (1 loop on hook), ch 2, sc 2 in the back bump of the 2nd ch from hook (wrist formed)
Row 14: ch 2, turn, sk 2 ch sts, sl st into 1st sc (thumb formed), ch 2, 1 hdc into the same st as sl st, hdc in next sc st
Row 15: turn, but do not ch 1, sk 1st hdc, sl st in the top of the next hdc

- FO.
- Darn the loose end into the hand.
- Set aside until Round 3 of the body.

LEFT HAND

Row 13: yo, pull through all three (1 loop on hook), ch 3, sl st in back bump of 2nd ch from hook (thumb formed), sc 2 in the back bump of the remaining ch (wrist formed)
Row 14: ch 2, turn, hdc 1 in ea of the 2 sc sts
Row 15: turn, but do not ch 1, sk 1st hdc, sl st in the top of the next hdc

- FO.
- Darn the loose end into the hand.
- Set aside until Round 3 of the body.

FEET and LEGS (Make 2)

- Working in continuous rounds
- Starting with the foot and working into the leg

Round 1: 6 sc in a magic ring (6)
Round 2: (sc inc in ea st) around (12)
Round 3: (sc in ea st) around (12)
Round 4: (sc2tog) six times (6)

- Tuck the end into the foot.
- Do not stuff.
- Pull up two more loops evenly spaced across the opening of the foot; this closes the foot and provides the loops needed to start the I-cord (3 loops on hook).

I-CORD LEGS

- Working in rows
- Do NOT turn

Row 1: Drop 2 loops (pinching them so they don't unravel), ch 1, pick up 2nd loop & ch 1, pick up last loop & ch 1
Row 2 - Row 17: repeat Row 1

- To finish, yo, pull through all three, cut yarn, yo, pull through one.
- Set aside until Round 15 of the body.

BODY

- Working from the neck down
- Working in continuous rounds

Round 1: sc 6 in a magic ring (6)
Round 2: (sc inc) around (12)
Round 3: sc 3, sc 3 while joining right arm, sc 3, sc 3 while joining left arm (12)
- Double-check your arms are placed correctly, with thumbs facing forward (your stitch marker is on his back.)
Round 4: (sc in ea st) around (12)
- Install cotter pin if jointing the neck.
Round 5: (sc in ea st) around (12)
Round 6: (sc in the next 3 sts, sc inc) around (15)
Round 7: (sc in ea st) around (15)
Round 8: (sc in the next 4 sts, sc inc) around (18)
Round 9: (sc in the next 5 sts, sc inc) around (21)
Round 10 - Round 11: (sc in ea st) around (21)
Round 12: (sc in the next 6 sts, sc inc) around (24)
Round 13: (sc in the next 7 sts, sc inc) around (27)
Round 14: (sc in ea st) around (27)
Round 15: sc 14, sc 2 while joining 1st leg, sc 5, sc 2 while joining 2nd leg, sc 4 (27)
Round 16: (sc in the next st, sc2tog) around (18)
- Stuff the body
Round 17: repeat round 16 (12)
Round 18: (sc2tog) around (6)

- FO & drawstring close.
- Sew the head to the body if you didn't joint the neck.

Floppy Monkey

MATERIALS:

- Worsted weight yarn (medium 4)
    - Red Heart Super Saver in Coral (14.5 g)
    - Red Heart Super Saver in Aran (11 g)
- 4 mm hook
- Stitch marker(s)
- Scissors
- Fiberfill
- 12 mm safety eyes in brown
- Doll-making needle
- Optional: one 3/32" x 1 ½" cotter pin, one 3/32" x 3/16" hitch pin clip, two 3/16" fender washers, two No. 6 countersunk finishing washers, and pliers for bending the cotter pin (if you are doing the jointed neck)

ABBREVIATIONS USED IN THIS FLOPPY:

Ch - Chain	PM - Place Marker	YO - Yarn Over
Dc - Double crochet	Sc - Single Crochet	
Ea - Each	Sc2tog - Single Crochet Two Together	
FO - Finish Off	Sk - Skip	
Hdc - Half Double Crochet	Sl st - Slip Stitch	
Inc - Increase	St(s) - Stitch or Stitches	

Floppy Monkey Teaches:

- Changing Colors - pg. 155
- Drop Stitch - pg. 40 & pg. 150
- Double Crochet stitch - pg. 152
- Rooting the ears - pg. 41

39

- Green marks eyes
- Blue marks drop stitch

First drop stitch one row down at marker

Complete as you would a single crochet stitch

Second drop stitch at same level as eye markers

Pull up to same height and complete sc stitch

Last drop stitch in the same space as the first

Complete stitch and remove the forehead marker

HEAD

- Working from the nose to the back of the head
- Working in continuous rounds
- Starting with the face color (Aran)

Round 1: sc 4 in a magic ring (4)
Round 2: (sc inc each st) around (8)
Round 3: (sc in the next st, sc inc) around (12)
Round 4: (sc in the next 2 sts, sc inc) around (16)
Round 5: (sc in the next 3 sts, sc inc) around (20)
Round 6: (sc in the next 4 sts, sc inc) around (24)
Round 7: sc in the next 3 sts, (1 hdc, hdc inc) three times, 1 hdc, sc in the next 7 sts, (sc2tog) two times, sc in remaining 3 sts (25)

- PM in base of 2nd and 2nd to last hdc sts of Round 7, and also in the middle of the hdc sts (this marks the center stitch of the forehead)

Round 8: (sc in ea st) around, in last st of round change to main color (25)

- Now working in main body color (Coral)

Round 9: sc 8, work a sc drop stitch in the next st of round 7, work a sc drop st directly below the middle hdc st of round 7, work one more sc drop st into the same st as the first sc drop st (you will have buried one st from round 8 beneath your drop stitches, sk that stitch and continue around) sc 16 (27)
Round 10: sc 9, sc2tog, sc 11, sc2tog, sc 3 (25)
Round 11: (sc in the next 3 sts, sc2tog) around (20)
Round 12: (sc in the next 2 sts, sc2tog) around (15)
Round 13: (sc in the next st, sc2tog) around (10)

- FO with a long tail.
- Place eyes at the base of the 2nd and 2nd-to-last hdc sts (where you placed your stitch markers).
- Place cotter pin or doll joint (if jointing the neck) at bottom/center between Round 7 & Round 8.
- Stuff the head.
- Use the long end for the drawstring close, but do not FO. Leave it to use to make the nostrils after placing the muzzle.
- Continue on to the muzzle.

MUZZLE

- With face-color yarn (Aran)
- Start and finish with long tail to use when sewing in place
- Working in continuous rounds

Round 1: 1 sc, 2 hdc, 2 sc, 2 hdc, 1 sc, into a magic ring (8)
Round 2: sc 1, (hdc inc) twice, sc 2, (hdc inc) twice, sc 1 (12)
Round 3: sc 1, (hdc inc) four times, sc 2, (hdc inc) four times, sc 1 (20)
Round 4: (sc in ea st) around (20)

- Sl st in next st and FO with a long tail to use to sew to the face.
- Do not stuff, or stuff lightly if needed.
- Set the muzzle over the point of the face & sew into place.
- Tack the eyes with the end from the muzzle.
- Add nostrils with the end from the drawstring close.
- Sew the nostrils as two vertical lines, over Round 2 and Round 3.

EARS (Make 2)

- Rooting the ears directly onto the head
- Starting and finishing with long tail to use in shaping
- Working in same color as face (Aran)

NOTE: Lefties will need to work the following two points in reverse, so the Right ear instructions for the Left, and vice versa.

- For **LEFT EAR** join with monkey facing you, in line with the bottom of his eye. Work in the row of the color change. Work up three stitches at the side of his face.
- For **RIGHT EAR** join with monkey facing you, in line with the top of his eye. Work in the row of the color change. Work down three stitches at the side of his face.

Row 1: sc & hdc in 1st st, dc 3 in next st, hdc & sc in the last st (7)

- FO and bring both tails in through the head entering in front of the same st as the 3 dc sts were worked.
- Exit through the same st and tie the ends together to secure the fold of the ear.
- Hide the ends inside the head.
- Set the head aside until Round 4 of the body (if jointing the neck) or until the body is completed (if sewing the head in place).

Rooting directly into the head

Root the sts for the ear over the next 3 sts of the head

Bring the end through in front/center of ear

Bring other end through the head and tie off

ARMS and HANDS (Make 2)

- Working in main color (Coral)
- Staring with the I-cord arm and working into the hand
- Do NOT turn while working the I-cord.
- Note: There is a left and right hand; make one of each.
- Finishing with a long tail. Bring tail up through arms and hide ends in the body. Ends have a way of working their way out of the cord; bringing them to the body eliminates this problem.

Row 1: ch 3
Row 2: Insert hook in 2nd ch from hook, yo, pull up loop, insert hook in 3rd ch from hook, yo, pull up loop (3 loops on hook)
Row 3: Drop 2 loops (pinching them so they don't unravel), ch 1, pick up 2nd loop & ch 1, pick up last loop & ch 1
Row 4 - Row 12: repeat Row 3

- Yo, and pull through all 3 loops of the I-cord (one loop on hook)
- FO with a long tail and leave it loose until after the hand is completed.
- Change color and begin on appropriate hand.

RIGHT HAND

- Starting and Finishing with a long tail
- Now working in hand color (Aran)

Row 13: ch 2, sc 2 in the back bump of the 2nd ch from hook (wrist formed)
Row 14: ch2, turn, sk 2 ch sts, sl st into 1st sc (thumb formed), ch 2, 1 hdc into the same st as sl st, hdc in next sc st
Row 15: turn, but do not ch 1, sk 1st hdc, sl st in the top of the next hdc

- FO.
- Darn the ends from the hand into the hand.
- Bring the I-cord end from the wrist up through the I-cord and tie at the horizontal bar at the top of the I-cord; leave loose end to hide in the body.
- Set aside until Round 3 of the body.

LEFT HAND

- Starting and Finishing with a long tail
- Now working in hand color (Aran)

Row 13: ch 3, sl st in back bump of 2nd ch from hook (thumb formed), sc 2 in the back bump of the remaining ch
Row 14: ch 2, turn, sk 2 ch sts, hdc 1 in ea of the 2 sc sts
Row 15: turn, but do not ch 1, sk 1st hdc, sl st in the top of the next hdc

- FO.
- Darn the ends from the hand into the hand.
- Bring the I-cord end from the wrist up through the I-cord and tie at the horizontal bar at the top of the I-cord; leave loose end to hide in the body.
- Set aside until Round 3 of the body.

Red Heart, Super Saver in Coffee

LEGS and FEET (Make 2)

- Working in main color (Coral)
- Starting with the I-cord leg and working into the foot
- Do NOT turn while working the I-cord.
- Note: There is a left and right foot; make one of each.
- Finishing with a long tail. Bring the tail up through the leg and hide the ends in the body. Ends have a way of working their way out of the I-cord; bringing them to the body eliminates this problem.

Row 1 - Row 3: Repeat Rows 1-3 of the Arms
Row 4 - Row 17: repeat Row 3

- Yo, and pull through all 3 loops of the I-cord (one loop on hook).
- FO with a long tail and leave it loose until after the foot is completed.
- Change color and start on appropriate foot.

RIGHT FOOT

- Starting and finishing with a long tail
- Now working in foot color (Aran)

Row 18: ch 2
Row 19: sc 2 in the 2nd ch from the hook, ch 3, turn (5)
Row 20: sc in the back bump of both the 2nd and 3rd ch from the hook, sc in ea of the remaining two sc sts, ch 2, turn
Row 21: hdc in ea of the 1st 2 sc sts (2)
Row 22 - 23: ch 1, turn (sc in ea st) across (2)
Row 24: turn, but do NOT ch, sk 1st st, sl st in the 2nd sc

- FO.
- Darn the ends from the foot into the foot.
- Bring the I-cord end from the ankle up through the I-cord and tie at the horizontal bar at the top of the I-cord; leave loose end to hide in the body.
- Set aside until Round 15 of the body.

LEFT FOOT

- Starting and finishing with a long tail
- Now working in foot color (Aran)

Row 18: ch 2
Row 19: sc 2 in the 2nd ch from the hook (2), ch 1, turn
Row 20: (sc in ea st) across (2), ch 3, turn
Row 21: sc in the back bump of both the 2nd and 3rd ch from the hook, sc in ea of the sc sts, ch 2, turn
Row 22: hdc in ea of the 1st two sc sts, leave the remaining sts unworked (2), ch 1, turn
Row 23: (sc in ea st) across (2)
Row 24: turn, but do NOT ch, sk 1st st, sl st in the 2nd sc

- FO.
- Darn the ends from the foot into the foot.
- Bring the I-cord end from the ankle up through the I-cord and tie at the horizontal bar at the top of the I-cord; leave loose end to hide in the body.
- Set aside until Round 15 of the body.

TAIL

- When working an I-cord, do NOT turn
- Working in the same color as the body (Coral)

Row 1: ch 3
Row 2: insert hook in 2nd ch from hook, yo, pull up loop, insert hook in 3rd ch from hook, yo, pull up loop (3 loops on hook)
Row 3: Drop 2 loops (pinching them so they don't unravel), ch 1, pick up 2nd loop & ch 1, pick up last loop & ch 1
Row 4 - Row 20: repeat Row 3

- Yo, and pull through all 3 loops.
- Yo, pull through one.
- FO with long end and bring it up through the center of the I-cord, knot on horizontal bar at the top of the I-cord and leave a length to hide inside of the body.
- Set aside until Round 15 of the body.

BODY

- Working in main color (Coral)
- Working from the neck down
- Working in continuous rounds

Round 1: sc 6 in a magic ring (6)
Round 2: (sc inc) around (12)
Round 3: sc 3, sc 3 while joining right arm, sc 3, sc 3 while joining left arm (12)
- Double-check that your arms are placed correctly, with thumbs facing forward (your stitch marker is on his back).
Round 4: (sc in ea st) around (12)
- Install cotter pin if jointing the neck.
Round 5: (sc in ea st) around (12)
Round 6: (sc in the next 3 sts, sc inc) around (15)
Round 7: (sc in ea st) around (15)
Round 8: (sc in the next 4 sts, sc inc) around (18)
Round 9: (sc in the next 5 sts, sc inc) around (21)
Round 10 - Round 11: (sc in ea st) around (21)
Round 12: (sc in the next 6 sts, sc inc) around (24)
Round 13: (sc in the next 7 sts, sc inc) around (27)
Round 14: (sc in ea st) around (27)
Round 15: sc 3, sc 3 while joining tail, sc 7, sc 3 while joining right leg, sc 5, sc 3 while joining left leg, sc 3 (27)
- Double-check that your legs are placed correctly, with big toes facing inward.
Round 16: (sc in the next st, sc2tog) around (18)
- Stuff the body
Round 17: repeat Round 16 (12)
Round 18: (sc2tog) around (6)

- FO & drawstring close.
- Sew the head to the body if you didn't joint the neck.

Floppy Panda Bear

MATERIALS:

- Worsted weight yarn (medium 4)
    - Red Heart Super Saver in White (13 g)
    - Red Heart Super Saver in Black (12 g)
- 4 mm hook
- Stitch marker(s)
- Scissors
- Fiberfill
- 12 mm safety eyes in brown
- Doll-making needle
- Optional: one 3/32" x 1 ½" cotter pin, one 3/32" x 3/16" hitch pin clip, two 3/16" fender washers, two No. 6 countersunk finishing washers, and pliers for bending the cotter pin (if you are doing the jointed neck)

ABBREVIATIONS USED IN THIS FLOPPY:

CC - Color Change
Ch - Chain
Ea - Each
FLO - Front Loop Only
FO - Finish Off
Hdc - Half Double Crochet

Inc - Increase
PM - Place Marker
Sc - Single Crochet
Sc2tog - Single Crochet Two Together
Sl st - Slip Stitch
St(s) - Stitch or Stitches

Yo - Yarn Over

Floppy Panda Bear Teaches:

- Changing Colors (mid-round) - pg. 155
- Carrying the yarn - pg. 155

47

EARS (Make 2)

- Working with Black yarn
- Working from top to base
- Working in continuous rounds

Round 1: sc 6 in a magic ring (6)
Round 2: (sc inc in ea st) around (12)
Round 3: (sc into ea st) around (12)

- FO.
- Do not stuff.
- Set aside until Round 10 of the head.

NOSE

- With Black yarn
- Starting and finishing with long tail to use when sewing in place

Row 1: sc 3 into magic ring, pull to close but do not join

- FO.
- Set aside until the head is complete.
- Sew in place with the bottom point of the nose at the center of the magic ring that was used to start the head.

HEAD

- Working from the nose to the back of the head
- Working in continuous rounds
- Starting with White yarn

Round 1: sc 6 in a magic ring (6)
Round 2: (sc inc in ea st) around (12)
Round 3 - Round 4: (sc in ea st) around (12)
Round 5: (in FLO sc in the next 2 sts, FLO sc inc) around (16)
Round 6: sc, cc to Black, sc 2, sc inc, sc 3, sc inc, cc to White, (sc 3, sc inc) twice (20)
Round 7: sc, cc to Black, sc 3, sc inc, sc 4, sc inc, cc to White, (sc 4, sc inc) twice (24)
Round 8: sc, cc to Black, sc 2, (1 hdc, hdc inc) three times, 1 hdc, sc 2, cc to White, sc in the next 5 sts, (sc2tog) two times, sc in remaining 3 sts (25)
- PM in base of 1st and last hdc sts of Round 8, and also in the middle of the hdc sts (this marks the center stitch of the forehead)
- FO Black yarn
Round 9: (sc in ea st) around (25)
Round 10: sc 1, sc 6 while joining ear, sc 1, using the forehead marker as guidance drop st 3 into center st of the nearest round of white (this will bury one st beneath the drop sts, skip that st), sc 1, sc 6 while joining ear, sc 9 (27)
Round 11: sc 9, sc2tog, sc 11, sc2tog, sc 3 (25)
Round 12: (sc in the next 3 sts, sc2tog) around (20)
Round 13: (sc in the next 2 sts, sc2tog) around (15)
Round 14: (sc in the next st, sc2tog) around (10)

- FO with a long tail.
- Place eyes at the base of the 1st and last hdc sts (where you placed your stitch markers).
- Place cotter pin (if jointing the neck) at bottom/center between Round 8 & Round 9.
- Stuff the head.
- Use the long end for the drawstring close.
- Use black yarn for needle sculpting to tuck the eyes, if desired
- Sew on the nose.
- Set the head aside until Round 4 of the body (if jointing the neck) or until the body is completed (if sewing the head in place).

HANDS and ARMS (Make 2)

- Working with Black yarn
- Working in continuous rounds
- Starting with the hand and working into the arm

Round 1: 6 sc in a magic ring (6)
Round 2 - Round 3: (sc in ea st) around (6)

- Tuck the end into the hand.
- Do not stuff.
- Pull up two more loops evenly spaced across the opening of the hand; this closes the hand and provides the loops needed to start the I-cord (3 loops on hook).

I-CORD ARMS

- Working in rows
- Do NOT turn

Row 1: Drop 2 loops (pinching them so they don't unravel), ch 1, pick up 2nd loop & ch 1, pick up last loop & ch 1
Row 2 - Row 12: repeat Row 1

- To finish, yo, pull through all three, cut yarn, yo, pull through one.
- Set aside until Round 3 of the body.

FEET and LEGS (Make 2)

- Working with Black yarn
- Working in continuous rounds
- Starting with the foot and working into the leg

Round 1: 6 sc in a magic ring (6)
Round 2: (sc inc in ea st) around (12)
Round 3: (sc in ea st) around (12)
Round 4: (sc2tog) six times (6)

- Tuck the end into the foot.
- Do not stuff.
- Pull up two more loops evenly spaced across the opening of the foot; this closes the foot and provides the loops needed to start the I-cord (3 loops on hook).

I-CORD LEGS

- Working in rows
- Do NOT turn

Row 1: Drop 2 loops (pinching them so they don't unravel), ch 1, pick up 2nd loop & ch 1, pick up last loop & ch 1
Row 2 - Row 17: repeat Row 1

- To finish, yo, pull through all three, cut yarn, yo, pull through one.
- Set aside until Round 15 of the body.

TAIL

- Working with White yarn

Row 1: sc, 6 hdc, sc in a magic ring (8)

- Pull magic ring closed but do not join.
- FO.
- Set aside until Round 15 of the body.

BODY

- Starting with Black yarn
- Working from the neck down
- Working in continuous rounds

Round 1: sc 6 in a magic ring (6)
Round 2: (sc inc) around (12)
Round 3: sc 3, sc 2 while joining 1st arm, sc 4, sc 2 while joining 2nd arm, sc 1 (12)
Round 4: (sc in ea st) around (12)
- Install cotter pin if jointing the neck
Round 5: (sc in ea st) around (12)
Round 6: (sc in the next 3 sts, sc inc) around (15)
- FO
- Sl st in next st
- Cc to White joining with a sc in the sl st
Round 7: (sc in ea st) around (15)
Round 8: (sc in the next 4 sts, sc inc) around (18)
Round 9: (sc in the next 5 sts, sc inc) around (21)
Round 10 - Round 11: (sc in ea st) around (21)
Round 12: (sc in the next 6 sts, sc inc) around (24)
Round 13: (sc in the next 7 sts, sc inc) around (27)
Round 14: (sc in ea st) around (27)
Round 15: sc 3, sc 2 while joining tail, sc 8, sc 2 while joining 1st leg, sc 5, sc 2 while joining 2nd leg, sc 5 (27)
Round 16: (sc in the next st, sc2tog) around (18)
- Stuff the body
Round 17: repeat round 16 (12)
Round 18: (sc2tog) around (6)

- FO & drawstring close.
- Sew the head to the body (if you didn't joint the neck).

Floppy Polar Bear

MATERIALS:

- Worsted weight yarn (medium 4)
  - Red Heart Super Saver in White (37.5 g)
  - Red Heart Super Saver in Black for nose (about a 30" length)
- 4 mm hook
- Stitch marker(s)
- Scissors
- Fiberfill
- 12 mm safety eyes in brown
- Doll-making needle
- Optional: one 3/32" x 1 ½" cotter pin, one 3/32" x 3/16" hitch pin clip, two 3/16" fender washers, two No. 6 countersunk finishing washers, and pliers for bending the cotter pin (if you are doing the jointed neck)

ABBREVIATIONS USED IN THIS FLOPPY:

Ch - Chain

Ea - Each

FLO - Front Loop Only

FO - Finish off

Hdc - Half Double Crochet

Inc - Increase

PM - Place Marker

Sc - Single crochet

Sc2tog - Single Crochet Two Together

St(s) - Stitch or Stitches

Yo - Yarn Over

Floppy Polar Bear Teaches:

- Joining the Toes - pg. 163

53

EARS (Make 2)

- Working from top to base
- Working in continuous rounds

Round 1: sc 6 in a magic ring (6)
Round 2: (sc inc in ea st) around (12)
Round 3: (sc into ea st) around (12)

- FO.
- Do not stuff.
- Set aside until Round 10 of the head.

NOSE

- Working with Black yarn
- Starting and finishing with long tail to use when sewing in place.

Row 1: sc 3 into magic ring, pull to close but do not join

- FO.
- Set aside until the head is complete.
- Sew in place with the bottom point of the nose at the center of the magic ring that was used to start the head.

HEAD

- Working from the nose to the back of the head
- Working in continuous rounds

Round 1: sc 6 in a magic ring (6)
Round 2: (sc inc in ea st) around (12)
Round 3 - Round 4: (sc in ea st) around (12)
Round 5: (in FLO sc in the next 2 sts, FLO sc inc) around (16)
Round 6: (sc in the next 3 sts, sc inc) around (20)
Round 7: (sc in the next 4 sts, sc inc) around (24)
Round 8: sc in the next 3 sts, (1 hdc, hdc inc) three times, 1 hdc, sc in the next 7 sts, (sc2tog) two times, sc in remaining 3 sts (25)
- PM in base of 1st and last hdc sts of Round 8
Round 9: (sc in ea st) around (25)
Round 10: sc 1, sc 6 while joining ear, sc 3, sc 6 while joining ear, sc 9 (25)
Round 11: (sc in ea st) around (25)
Round 12: (sc in the next 3 sts, sc2tog) around (20)
Round 13: (sc in the next 2 sts, sc2tog) around (15)
Round 14: (sc in the next st, sc2tog) around (10)

- FO with a long tail.
- Place eyes at the base of the 1st and last hdc sts (where you placed your stitch markers).
- Place cotter pin (if jointing the neck) at bottom/center between Round 8 & Round 9.
- Stuff the head.
- Use the long end for the drawstring close and for needle sculpting to tuck the eyes, if desired.
- Sew on the nose.
- Set the head aside until Round 4 of the body (if jointing the neck) or until the body is completed (if sewing the head in place).

TOES (Make 3 per foot: Make 2 and FO, Make 1 and do NOT FO)

- Working in continuous rounds

Round 1: 4 sc in a magic ring (4)
Round 2: (sc inc in ea st) around (8)
Round 3: (sc in ea st) around (8)
Round 4: (sc2tog) around (4)

- Tuck the end into the toe.
- Do not stuff.
- FO on first two toes.
- Do NOT FO on third toe; continue on to the foot.

PUTTING TOES TOGETHER AND FORMING THE FOOT (Make 4)

- With the last toe made still on the hook (now being referred to as the first toe) and using its working yarn.

Round 5: sc in two sc sts of middle toe, sc in 4 sc sts of last toe, moving back along the other side of the toes, sc in 2 sc sts of the middle toe, sc in the 4 sc sts of the first toe (12)
Round 6: (sc inc in ea st) aorund (24)
Round 7: (sc in ea st) around (24)
Round 8: (sc2tog) around (12)
Round 9: (sc2tog) around (6)

- Do NOT FO.
- Lightly stuff the foot.
- Pull up two more loops evenly spaced across the opening of the foot; this closes the foot and provides the loops needed to start the I-cord (3 loops on the hook).
- Move on to the arm or leg.

I-CORD ARMS (Make 2)

- Working in rows
- Do NOT turn

Row 1: Drop 2 loops (pinching them so they don't unravel), ch 1, pick up 2nd loop & ch 1, pick up last loop & ch 1
Row 2 - Row 12: repeat Row 1

- To finish, yo, pull through all three, cut yarn, yo, pull through one.
- Set aside until Round 3 of the body.

I-CORD LEGS (Make 2)

- Working in rows
- Do NOT turn

Row 1: Drop 2 loops (pinching them so they don't unravel), ch 1, pick up 2nd loop & ch 1, pick up last loop & ch 1
Row 2 - Row 15: repeat Row 1

- To finish, yo, pull through all three, cut yarn, yo, pull through one.
- Set aside until Round 15 of the body.

TAIL

Row 1: sc, 6 hdc, sc in a magic ring (8)

- Pull magic ring closed but do not join.
- FO.
- Set aside until Round 15 of the body.

BODY

- Working from the neck down
- Working in continuous rounds

Round 1: sc 6 in a magic ring (6)
Round 2: (sc inc) around (12)
Round 3: sc 3, sc 2 while joining 1st arm, sc 4, sc 2 while joining 2nd arm, sc 1 (12)
Round 4: (sc in ea st) around (12)
- Install cotter pin if jointing the neck
Round 5: (sc in ea st) around (12)
Round 6: (sc in the next 3 sts, sc inc) around (15)
Round 7: (sc in ea st) around (15)
Round 8: (sc in the next 4 sts, sc inc) around (18)
Round 9: (sc in the next 5 sts, sc inc) around (21)
Round 10 - Round 11: (sc in ea st) around (21)
Round 12: (sc in the next 6 sts, sc inc) around (24)
Round 13: (sc in the next 7 sts, sc inc) around (27)
Round 14: (sc in ea st) around (27)
Round 15: sc 3, sc 2 while joining tail, sc 8, sc 2 while joining 1st leg, sc 5, sc 2 while joining 2nd leg, sc 5 (27)
Round 16: (sc in the next st, sc2tog) around (18)
- Stuff the body
Round 17: repeat round 16 (12)
Round 18: (sc2tog) around (6)

- FO & drawstring close.
- Sew the head to the body if you didn't joint the neck.

Floppy Sloth

MATERIALS:

- Worsted weight yarn (medium 4)
  - Red Heart Super Saver in Cafe Latte (18.5 g)
  - Red Heart Super Saver in Aran (13.5 g)
- 4 mm hook
- Stitch marker(s)
- Scissors
- Fiberfill
- 12 mm safety eyes in brown
- Doll-making needle
- Optional: one 3/32" x 1 ½" cotter pin, one 3/32" x 3/16" hitch pin clip, two 3/16" fender washers, two No. 6 countersunk finishing washers, and pliers for bending the cotter pin (if you are doing the jointed neck)

ABBREVIATIONS USED IN THIS FLOPPY:

Cc - Change Color

Ch - Chain

Dc - Double Crochet

Ea - Each

FO - Finish Off

Hdc - Half Double Crochet

Inc - Increase

PM - Place Marker

Sc - Single Crochet

Sc2tog - Single Crochet Two Together

St(s) - Stitch or Stitches

Yo - Yarn Over

Floppy Sloth Reviews:
- Joining Toes – pg. 163
- Drop Stitch – pg. 150
- Changing Colors – pg. 155
- Carrying the yarn – pg. 155

NOSE

- With same color as eye patches (Cafe Latte)
- Starting and finishing with long tail to use when sewing in place

Row 1: working into a magic ring ch 2, dc 4, pull to close but do not join

- FO.
- Set aside until the head is complete.
- Sew in place with the bottom point of the nose at the center of the magic ring that was used to start the head.

HEAD

- Working from the nose to the back of the head
- Working in continuous rounds
- Starting with face color (Aran)

Round 1: sc 4 in a magic ring (4)
Round 2: (sc inc in each st) around (8)
Round 3: (sc in the next st, sc inc) around (12)
Round 4: (sc in the next 2 sts, sc inc) around (16)
Round 5: (sc in the next 3 sts, sc inc) around (20)
Round 6: sc, cc to Cafe Latte, sc 3, sc inc, sc 4, sc inc, cc back to face color, (sc 4, sc inc) two times (24)
Round 7: sc, cc to Cafe Latte, sc 2, (1 hdc, hdc inc) three times, 1 hdc, sc 2, cc back to face color, FO Cafe Latte yarn sc 5, (sc2tog) two times, sc 3 (25)
- PM in 1st and last hdc sts and mark the center of the hdc sts of Round 7
Round 8: (sc in ea st) around (25)
Round 9: sc 8, using the forehead marker as guidance drop st 3 into center st of the nearest round of Aran/face color (this will bury one st beneath the drop sts, skip that st), sc 16, cc to body color (Cafe Latte) on last st (27)
- FO face color (Aran)
- Now working in body color (Cafe Latte)
Round 10: sc 9, sc2tog, sc 11, sc2tog, sc 3 (25)
Round 11: (sc in the next 3 sts, sc2tog) around (20)
Round 12: (sc in the next 2 sts, sc2tog) around (15)
Round 13: (sc in the next st, sc2tog) around (10)

- FO with a long tail.
- Place eyes at the base of the 1st and last hdc sts (where you placed your stitch markers).
- Place cotter pin (if jointing the neck) at bottom/center between Round 8 & Round 9.
- Stuff the head.
- Use the long end for the drawstring close and for needle sculpting to tuck the eyes, if desired.
- Sew on the nose.
- Set the head aside until Round 4 of the body (if jointing the neck) or until the body is completed (if sewing the head in place).

TOES (Make 3 per foot)

- Working in continuous rounds
- Working in claw color (Aran)

Round 1: 4 sc in a magic ring (4)
Round 2 - Round 5: (sc in ea st) around (4)

- Tuck the end into the toe.
- Do not stuff.
- FO.

Red Heart, Super Saver in Oatmeal

PUTTING TOES TOGETHER AND FORMING THE FOOT (Make 4)

- Join to 1st claw with a sc using the body-colored yarn (Cafe Latte)

Round 6: sc in two sc sts of 1st toe, sc in 2 sc sts of the middle toe, sc in the 4 sc sts of the last toe, moving back along the other side of the toes, sc in the remaining 2 sts of the middle toe, sc in the remaining 2 sts of the 1st toe (12)
- Now working in continuous rounds
Round 7: (sc in ea st) around (12)
Round 8: (sc2tog) around (6)

- Do NOT FO.
- Hide the ends inside, but do not stuff the foot.
- Pull up two more loops evenly spaced across the opening of the foot; this closes the foot and provides the loops needed to start the I-cord (3 loops on the hook)
- Move on to the arm or leg.

I-CORD ARMS (Make 2)

- Working in rows
- Do NOT turn

Row 1: Drop 2 loops, pinching them so they don't unravel, ch 1, pick up 2nd loop & ch 1, pick up last loop & ch 1
Row 2 - Row 12: repeat Row 1

- To finish, yo, pull through all three, cut yarn, yo, pull through one.
- Set aside until Round 3 of the body.

I-CORD LEGS (Make 2)

- Working in rows
- Do NOT turn

Row 1: Drop 2 loops (pinch them so they don't unravel), ch 1, pick up 2nd loop & ch 1, pick up last loop & ch 1
Row 2 - Row 15: repeat Row 1

- To finish, yo, pull through all three, cut yarn, yo, pull through one.
- Set aside until Round 15 of the body.

BODY

- Working from the neck down
- Working in continuous rounds
- Working in body color (Cafe Latte)

Round 1: sc 6 in a magic ring (6)
Round 2: (sc inc) around (12)
Round 3: sc 3, sc 2 while joining 1st arm, sc 4, sc 2 while joining 2nd arm, sc 1 (12)
Round 4: (sc in ea st) around (12)
- Install cotter pin if jointing the neck
Round 5: (sc in ea st) around (12)
Round 6: (sc in the next 3 sts, sc inc) around (15)
Round 7: (sc in ea st) around (15)
Round 8: (sc in the next 4 sts, sc inc) around (18)
Round 9: (sc in the next 5 sts, sc inc) around (21)
Round 10 - Round 11: (sc in ea st) around (21)
Round 12: (sc in the next 6 sts, sc inc) around (24)
Round 13: (sc in the next 7 sts, sc inc) around (27)
Round 14: (sc in ea st) around (27)
Round 15: sc 14, sc 2 while joining 1st leg, sc 5, sc 2 while joining 2nd leg, sc 4 (27)
Round 16: (sc in the next st, sc2tog) around (18)
- Stuff the body
Round 17: repeat round 16 (12)
Round 18: (sc2tog) around (6)

- FO & drawstring close.
- Sew the head to the body if you didn't joint the neck.

TAIL

- Working in body color (Cafe Latte)
- Rooting the tail directly to the body on same round as legs (Round 15)
- Inserting hook pointing downwards through the center stitch on the bum.

Row 1: join with sc st, ch 2, sc in same st

- FO.
- Hide ends in the body, working on the underside of the same stitch.

Floppy Elephant

MATERIALS:

- Worsted weight yarn (medium 4)
    - Red Heart Super Saver in Dusty Grey (41.5 g)
- 4 mm hook
- Stitch marker(s)
- Scissors
- Fiberfill
- 12 mm safety eyes in brown
- Doll-making needle
- Optional: one 3/32" x 1 ½" cotter pin, one 3/32" x 3/16" hitch pin clip, two 3/16" fender washers, two No. 6 countersunk finishing washers, and pliers for bending the cotter pin (if you are doing the jointed neck)

ABBREVIATIONS USED IN THIS FLOPPY:

BLO - Back Loop Only

Ch - Chain

Dc - Double Crochet

Ea - Each

FO - Finish Off

Hdc - Half Double Crochet

Inc - Increase

PM - Place Marker

Sc - Single Crochet

Sc2tog - Single Crochet Two Together

Sl st - Slip Stitch

St(s) - Stitch or Stitches

Yo - Yarn Over

Floppy Elephant Teaches:

- Back Loop Only – pg. 147

EARS (Make 2)

Row 1: ch 12, join with sl st (12)
Round 2: ch 1, sc in the back bump of the same st as the join and each of the remaining 11 sts (12)
  • From this point on, working in continuous rounds
Round 3: (sc in the next 2 sts, sc inc) around (16)
Round 4: (sc in the next 3 sts, sc inc) around (20)
Round 5: (sc in the next 4 sts, sc inc) around (24)
Round 6: (sc inc) six times, sc in the next 12 sts, (sc inc) in remaining 6 sts. (36)
Round 7: (sc in ea st) around (36)
Round 8: sc in the first 15 sts, (sc2tog) three times, sc in the remaining 15 sts (33)
Round 9: sc in the first 13 sts, (sc2tog) three times, sc in the remaining 14 sts (30)
Round 10: fold in half and close with 14 sl sts (14)

  • FO and hide the end inside the ear.
  • Do not stuff.
  • Set aside until Round 23 of the head.

Insert hook through both layers and yarn over

Pull through all to complete a slip stitch

HEAD

  • Working from the trunk to the back of the head
  • Working in continuous rounds

Round 1: sc 4 in a magic ring (4)
Round 2 - Round 8: (sc in ea st) around (4)
Round 9: (sc in the next st, sc inc) around (6)
Round 10 - Round 11: (sc in ea st) around (6)
Round 12: (sc in the next two sts, sc inc) around (8)
Round 13 - Round 14: (sc in ea st) around (8)
Round 15: (sc in the next st, sc inc) around (12)
Round 16 - Round 17: (sc in ea st) around (12)
Round 18: (sc in the next 2 sts, sc inc) around (16)
Round 19: (sc in the next 3 sts, sc inc) around (20)
Round 20: (sc in the next 4 sts, sc inc) around (24)
Round 21: sc in the next 3 sts, (1 hdc, 2 hdc) three times, 1 hdc, sc in the next 7 sts, (sc2tog) two times, sc in remaining 3 sts (25)
  • PM in base of 1st and last hdc sts of Round 21
Round 22: (sc in ea st) around (25)
Round 23: sc 6 while joining ear, sc 5, sc 6 while joining ear, sc 8 (25)
Round 24: (sc in ea st) around (25)
Round 25: (sc in the next 3 sts, sc2tog) around (20)
Round 26: (sc in the next 2 sts, sc2tog) around (15)
Round 27: (sc in the next st, sc2tog) around (10)

  • FO with a long tail.
  • Place eyes at the base of the 1st and last hdc sts (where you placed your stitch markers).
  • Place cotter pin (if jointing the neck) at bottom/center between Round 22 and Round 23.
  • Stuff the head, leaving the trunk unstuffed.
  • Use the long end for the drawstring close and for needle sculpting to tuck the eyes, if desired.
  • If desired, tack the trunk up with one or two stitches, with the tip of the trunk in the center of his face.
  • Set the head aside until Round 4 of the body (if jointing the neck) or until the body is completed (if sewing the head in place).

BOTTOM LIP

- Rooting around the posts of Round 18 at the center three stitches at the base of the trunk
- Insert the hook pointing towards the front of the face

Row 1: sc in the 1st st, hdc, dc, hdc, in the second st, sc in the 3rd st

- FO.
- Shape the lip by tacking the corners of the mouth; hide the ends inside the head.

Rooting directly into the head

Root the sts for the lip over the next 3 sts of the head

Use the loose ends to tack corners of the lip in place

The lip should form a half circle

HANDS and FEET (Make 4)

- Working in continuous rounds

Round 1: sc 6 in a magic ring (6)
Round 2: (sc inc in ea st) around (12)
Round 3: (sc in BLO of ea st) around (12)
Round 4 - Round 5: (sc in ea st) around (12)
Round 6: (sc2tog) six times (6)

- Tuck the end into the foot. Lightly stuff.
- Pull up three loops evenly spaced across the top opening of the foot; this closes the foot and provides the 3 starting loops for your I-cord.
- Do not FO; use the three loops to start the arms/legs.

I-CORD ARMS and LEGS (Make 4)

- Working in rows
- Do NOT turn

Row 1: Drop 2 loops (pinching them so they don't unravel), ch 1, pick up 2nd loop & ch 1, pick up last loop & ch 1
Row 2 - Row 12: repeat Row 1

- To finish, yo, pull through all three, yo, pull through one.
- Set aside until Round 15 of the body.

BODY

- Working from the neck down
- Working in continuous rounds

Round 1: sc 6 in a magic ring (6)
Round 2: (sc inc) around (12)
Round 3: sc 3, sc 2 while joining 1st arm, sc 4, sc 2 while joining 2nd arm, sc 1 (12)
Round 4: (sc in ea st) around (12)
- Install cotter pin if jointing the neck
Round 5: (sc in ea st) around (12)
Round 6: (sc in the next 3 sts, sc inc) around (15)
Round 7: (sc in ea st) around (15)
Round 8: (sc in the next 4 sts, sc inc) around (18)
Round 9: (sc in the next 5 sts, sc inc) around (21)
Round 10 - Round 11: (sc in ea st) around (21)
Round 12: (sc in the next 6 sts, sc inc) around (24)
Round 13: (sc in the next 7 sts, sc inc) around (27)
Round 14: (sc in ea st) around (27)
Round 15: sc 14, sc 2 while joining 1st leg, sc 5, sc 2 while joining 2nd leg, sc 4 (27)
Round 16: (sc in the next st, sc2tog) around (18)
- Stuff the body
Round 17: repeat round 16 (12)
Round 18: (sc2tog) around (6)

- FO & drawstring close.
- Sew the head to the body if you didn't joint the neck.

TAIL

- Start with about a two foot length of yarn.
- Fold in half.
- Insert hook through the stitch in the center of the bum on Round 16.
- Pull yarn through at the half-way fold point in the yarn.

Row 1: with both strands of yarn ch 6

- Yo, pull through all the way.
- Push your crochet hook through the last chain stitch of the tail.
- Pull through 2 more 6″ strands, folded in half. This creates a loop. Pull all ends through the loop and pull tight.
- Cut to desired length, and pull the yarn plies apart.

For the end of the tail, pull through two more stands

Pull all ends through the loop to create the tail fringe

Floppy Pig

MATERIALS:

- Worsted weight yarn (medium 4)
  - Red Heart Super Saver in Baby Pink (32.5 g)
- 4 mm hook
- Stitch marker(s)
- Scissors
- Fiberfill
- 12 mm safety eyes in brown
- Doll-making needle
- Optional: one 3/32" x 1 ½" cotter pin, one 3/32" x 3/16" hitch pin clip, two 3/16" fender washers, two No. 6 countersunk finishing washers, and pliers for bending the cotter pin (if you are doing the jointed neck)

ABBREVIATIONS USED IN THIS FLOPPY:

BLO - Back Loop Only
Ch - Chain
Ea - Each
FLO - Front Loop Only
FO - Finish Off
Hdc - Half Double Crochet

Inc - Increase
PM - Place Marker
Sc - Single Crochet
Sc2tog - Single Crochet Two Together
Sk - Skip Stitch
Sl st - Slip Stitch

St(s) - Stitch or Stitches
Yo - Yarn Over

Floppy Pig Teaches:

- Short Rows - pg. 157
- Sc2tog (Regular) - pg. 150

EARS (Make 2)

- Working from top to base
- Working in continuous rounds and short rows
- Ch 1 to turn does NOT count as a stitch.

Round 1: sc 4 in a magic ring (4)
Round 2: (sc in the next st, sc inc) around (6)
Round 3: (sc in the next 2 sts, sc inc) twice (8)
Round 4: (sc in the next 3 sts, sc inc) twice (10)
Round 5: (sc in the next 4 sts, sc inc) twice (12)
Row 6: sc 6, leave remaining 6 sts unworked, ch 1, turn (6)
Row 7: Sc in next 6, ch 1 turn (6)
Round 8: Sc in next 6, do not turn, sc2tog over the end of the two rows just completed, sc in the remain 6 sts from round 5, sc2tog over the end st of round 7 and the first st of round 8, ch1, do not turn (14)
Round 9: (sc in ea st) around (14)

- Sl st
- FO.
- Do not stuff.
- Set aside until Round 10 of the head.

HEAD

- Working from the snout to the back of the head
- Working in continuous rounds

Round 1: sc 6 in a magic ring (6)
Round 2: (sc inc in each st) around (12)
Round 3: (in BLO sc in ea st) around (12)
Round 4: (sc in ea st) around (12)
Round 5: (in FLO sc in the next 2 sts, 2 sc in the next st) around (16)
Round 6: (sc in the next 3 sts, sc inc) around (20)
Round 7: (sc in the next 4 sts, sc inc) around (24)
Round 8: sc in the next 3 sts, (1 hdc, 2 hdc) three times, 1 hdc, sc in the next 7 sts, (sc2tog) two times, sc in remaining 3 sts (25)
- PM in base of 1st and last hdc sts of Round 8
Round 9: (sc in ea st) around (25)
Round 10: sc 1, sc 7 while joining ear, sc 2, sc 7 while joining ear, sc 8 (25)
- Double-check ear placement (they should be pointing forward and slanting in towards the face).
Round 11: (sc in ea st) around (25)
Round 12: (sc in the next 3 sts, sc2tog) around (20)
Round 13: (sc in the next 2 sts, sc2tog) around (15)
Round 14: (sc in the next st, sc2tog) around (10)

- FO with a long tail.
- Place eyes at the base of the 1st and last hdc sts (where you placed your stitch markers).
- Place cotter pin (if jointing the neck) at bottom/center between Round 8 & Round 9.
- Stuff the head.
- Use the long end for the drawstring close and for needle sculpting to tuck the eyes, if desired.
- Set the head aside until Round 4 of the body (if jointing the neck) or until the body is completed (if sewing the head in place).

TOES (Make 2 per foot: Make 1 and FO, Make 1 and do NOT FO)

- Working in continuous rounds

Round 1: sc 4 in a magic ring (4)
Round 2: (sc in ea st) around (4)
Round 3: (sc in the next st, sc inc) around (6)

- Do not stuff the toes.
- FO on first toe.
- Do NOT FO on second toe; continue onto the foot.

PUTTING TOES TOGETHER AND FORMING THE FOOT (Make 4)

- With the last toe made still on the hook

Round 4: attach both pieces in center with 2 sc
Round 5: (sc in ea st) around the outside of the hoof (8)
Round 6: (sc in the next 2 sts, sc2tog) around (6)

- Do NOT FO.
- Tuck the ends inside of the foot. Do not stuff,
- Pull up two more loops evenly spaced across the opening of the foot; this closes the foot and provides the loops needed to start the I-cord (3 loops on the hook).
- Move on to the arm or leg.

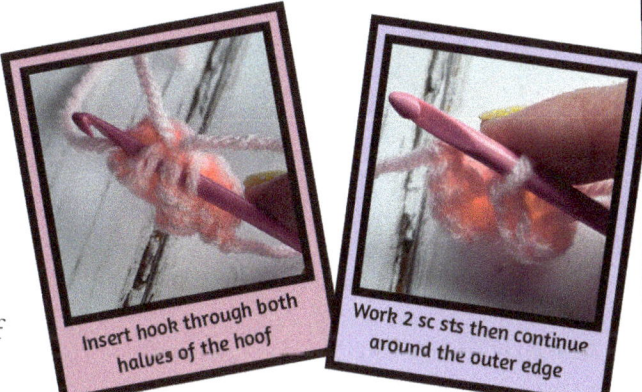

Insert hook through both halves of the hoof

Work 2 sc sts then continue around the outer edge

I-CORD ARMS (Make 2)

- Working in rows
- Do NOT turn

Row 1: Drop 2 loops (pinching them so they don't unravel), ch 1, pick up 2nd loop & ch 1, pick up last loop & ch 1
Row 2 - Row 9: repeat Row 1

- To finish, yo, pull through all three, cut yarn, yo, pull through one.
- Set aside until Round 3 of the body.

I-CORD LEGS (Make 2)

- Working in rows
- Do NOT turn

Row 1: Drop 2 loops (pinching them so they don't unravel), ch 1, pick up 2nd loop & ch 1, pick up last loop & ch 1
Row 2 - Row 15: repeat Row 1

- To finish, yo, pull through all three, cut yarn, yo, pull through one.
- Set aside until Round 15 of the body.

BODY

- Working from the neck down
- Working in continuous rounds

Round 1: sc 6 in a magic ring (6)
Round 2: (sc inc) around (12)
Round 3: sc 3, sc 2 while joining 1st arm, sc 4, sc 2 while joining 2nd arm, sc 1 (12)
Round 4: (sc in ea st) around (12)
- Install cotter pin if jointing the neck
Round 5: (sc in ea st) around (12)
Round 6: (sc in the next 3 sts, sc inc) around (15)
Round 7: (sc in ea st) around (15)
Round 8: (sc in the next 4 sts, sc inc) around (18)
Round 9: (sc in the next 5 sts, sc inc) around (21)
Round 10 - Round 11: (sc in ea st) around (21)
Round 12: (sc in the next 6 sts, sc inc) around (24)
Round 13: (sc in the next 7 sts, sc inc) around (27)
Round 14: (sc in ea st) around (27)
Round 15: sc 14, sc 2 while joining 1st leg, sc 5, sc 2 while joining 2nd leg, sc 4 (27)
Round 16: (sc in the next st, sc2tog) around (18)
- Stuff the body
Round 17: repeat round 16 (12)
Round 18: (sc2tog) around (6)

- FO & drawstring close.
- Sew the head to the body if you didn't joint the neck.

TAIL

- Attach to the bum with a sc at the back and center of Round 15.

Row 1: ch 10, turn
- working in back bump of chain
Row 2: sk the first ch st, sc 2 in ea ch st (18)

- Hide the ends inside the body.

MATERIALS:

- Worsted weight yarn (medium 4)
  - Red Heart Super Saver in Lemon (19.5 g)
  - Red Heart Super Saver in Pumpkin (4 g)
- 4 mm hook
- Stitch marker(s)
- Scissors
- Fiberfill
- 12 mm safety eyes in brown
- Doll-making needle
- Optional: one 3/32" x 1 ½" cotter pin, one 3/32" x 3/16" hitch pin clip, two 3/16" fender washers, two No. 6 countersunk finishing washers, and pliers for bending the cotter pin (if you are doing the jointed neck)

ABBREVIATIONS USED IN THIS FLOPPY:

BLO - Back Loop Only

Ch - Chain

Dc - Double Crochet

Ea - Each

FO - Finish Off

Hdc - Half Double Crochet

Inc - Increase

PM - Place Marker

Sc - Single Crochet

Sc2tog - Single Crochet Two Together

Sk - Skip

Sl st - Slip Stitch

St(s) - Stitch or Stitches

Tr - Treble

Yo - Yarn Over

Floppy Duck Teaches:

- Treble Stitch - pg. 153
- Crocheting the ends of a row - pg. 158

HEAD

- Working from the beak to the back of the head
- Starting with the beak color (Pumpkin)
- Working in continuous rounds

Round 1: sc 4 in a magic ring (4)
Round 2: (sc inc in each st) around (8)
Round 3 - Round 4: (sc in ea st) around (8)
Round 5: (sc in the next st, sc inc) around (12)
Round 6: (sc in ea st) around (12)
Round 7: (sc in the next 2 sts, sc inc) around (16)
- Sl st in next st and FO
- Join with a sc in any st
- Working with main color (Lemon)
Round 8: (sc in the next 3 sts, sc inc) around (20)
Round 9: (sc in the next 4 sts, sc inc) around (24)
Round 10: sc in the next 3 sts, (1 hdc, 2 hdc) three times, 1 hdc, sc in the next 7 sts, (sc2tog) two times, sc in remaining 3 sts (25)
- PM in base of 1st and last hdc sts of Round 10
Round 11 - Round 13: (sc in ea st) around (25)
Round 14: (sc in the next 3 sts, sc2tog) around (20)
Round 15: (sc in the next 2 sts, sc2tog) around (15)
Round 16: (sc in the next st, sc2tog) around (10)

- FO with a long tail.
- Place eyes at the base of the 1st and last hdc sts (where you placed your stitch markers).
- Place cotter pin (if jointing the neck) at bottom/center between Round 11 & Round12.
- Stuff the head, lightly stuffing the beak area.
- Use the long end for the drawstring close and for needle sculpting to tuck the eyes, if desired.
- Set the head aside until Round 4 of the body (if jointing the neck) or until the body is completed (if sewing the head in place).

FEET (Make 2)

- Starting with a long tail to use for darning
- Working with Orange yarn (Pumpkin)

Row 1: ch 4, working in the back bumps of ch, sl st in closest ch to hook, sl st in the next ch, sc in ea of the last 2 chains (1st toe complete)

Row 2: ch 1, turn, sc in ea of the next 2 sc, ch 3, working in the back bumps of ch, sl st in closest ch to hook, sl st in next 2 chains, sc in the next 2 sc (2nd toe complete)

Row 3: ch 1, turn, sc in the next 2 sc, ch 2, working in the back bumps of the ch, sl st in the closest ch to the hook, sl st in the next ch, sc in the next 2 sc (3rd toe complete)

Row 4: Working across the top of the ankle, insert hook, yo, pull up loop under middle toe, insert hook in corner st, yo, pull up loop (3 loops on hook)

- Use 3 loops on hook to begin I-cord.
- Do NOT finish off.
- Use working yarn to move onto the legs.

I-CORD LEGS (Make 2)

- Beginning with 3 loops on hook

Row 1: Drop 2 loops (pinching them so they don't unravel), ch 1, pick up 2nd loop & ch 1, pick up last loop & ch 1

Row 2 - Row 10: repeat Row 1

- To finish, yo, pull through all three, yo, pull through one.
- Use the end at the ankle to darn into the foot.
- Set aside until Round 15 of the body.

BODY

- Working from the neck down
- Working in continuous rounds
- Working with Yellow yarn (Lemon)

Round 1: sc 6 in a magic ring (6)
Round 2: (sc inc) around (12)
Round 3 - Round 4: (sc in ea st) around (12)
- Install cotter pin if jointing the neck

Round 5: (sc in ea st) around (12)
Round 6: (sc in the next 3 sts, sc inc) around (15)
Round 7: (sc in ea st) around (15)
Round 8: (sc in the next 4 sts, sc inc) around (18)
Round 9: (sc in the next 5 sts, sc inc) around (21)
Round 10 - Round 11: (sc in ea st) around (21)
Round 12: (sc in the next 6 sts, sc inc) around (24)
Round 13: (sc in the next 7 sts, sc inc) around (27)
Round 14: (sc in ea st) around (27)
Round 15: sc 14, sc 2 while joining 1st leg, sc 5, sc 2 while joining 2nd leg, sc 4 (27)
Round 16: (sc in the next st, sc2tog) around (18)
- Stuff the body

Round 17: repeat round 16 (12)
Round 18: (sc2tog) around (6)

- FO & drawstring close.
- Sew the head to the body if you didn't joint the neck.

WINGS (Make 2)

- Working in rows
- Working with Yellow yarn (Lemon)
- Ch 1 to turn does not count as a stitch

Row 1: ch 15 (15)
Row 2: turn, working in the back bumps of the ch, sk 1, sl st, sc, hdc 2 in next st, hdc in ea of the next 8 sts, sc in ea of the next 3 sts (15)
- Working in BLO on every stitch for the rest of the wing

Row 3: ch 1, turn, sc in ea of the next 3 sts, hdc in ea of the next 7 sts, sc in the next st, sl st in the next st, leave remaining sts unworked (12)
Row 4: ch 1, turn, sk 1, sc, hdc in ea of the next 7 sts, sc in ea of the remaining 3 sts (11)
Row 5: ch 1, turn, sc in ea of the next 3 sts, hdc in ea of the next 4 sts, sc, sl st, leave remaining sts unworked (9)
Row 6: ch 1, turn, sk 1, sc, hdc in ea of the next 4 sts, sc in ea of the remaining 3 sts (8)
Row 7: to pull in the pleats of the wing, place 3 sc sts evenly spaced up the inside edge of the wing. Place one in ea turning ch, and one in the corner at the beginning of the original starting ch (3)

- FO with a long tail to use to sew the wings to the sides over Rounds 5 to 7.

TAIL

- Working in body color (Lemon)
- Rooting tail directly to the body on same round as legs (round 15)
- Inserting the hook pointing downwards through the center stitch on the bum

Row 1: join with sl st, ch 2, (2 dc, tr, 2dc) through same stitch as sl st, ch 2, sl st in same stitch

- FO.
- Hide the ends inside the body.

Floppy Bumble Bee

MATERIALS:

- Worsted weight yarn (medium 4)
    - Red Heart Super Saver in Black (17 g)
    - Red Heart Super Saver in White (4 g)
    - Red Heart Super Saver in Saffron (7.5 g)
- 4 mm hook
- Stitch marker(s)
- Scissors
- Fiberfill
- 12 mm safety eyes in brown
- Doll-making needle
- Optional: one 3/32" x 1 ½" cotter pin, one 3/32" x 3/16" hitch pin clip, two 3/16" fender washers, two No. 6 countersunk finishing washers, and pliers for bending the cotter pin (if you are doing the jointed neck)

ABBREVIATIONS USED IN THIS FLOPPY:

Cc - Change Color

Ch - Chain

Dc - Double Crochet

Ea - Each

FO - Finish Off

Hdc - Half Double Crochet

Inc - Increase

PM - Place Marker

Sc - Single Crochet

Sc2tog - Single Crochet Two Together

Sl st - Slip Stitch

St(s) - Stitch or Stitches

Tr - Treble

Yo - Yarn Over

Floppy Bumble Bee Teaches:

- Velcroing - pg. 86

ANTENNA (Make 2)

Special Stitch Instructions for Puff Stitch:
Yo, insert in back bump of the 2nd ch from hook, yo, pull up loop, yo, insert hook into same st, yo, pull up loop, yo, pull through all 5 loops on the hook.

- Working with Black yarn
- Starting and finishing with a long tail for tying off inside head

Row 1: ch 6
Row 2: puff st in the 2nd ch from the hook, sl st in the same st, sc 5 AROUND the ch, sc in the back bump of the last ch st.

- FO.
- Set aside until round 8 of the head.

HEAD

- Working from the nose to the back of the head
- Working in continuous rounds
- Starting with Yellow yarn (Saffron)

Round 1: sc 6 into a magic ring (6)
Round 2: (sc inc in ea st) around (12)
Round 3: (sc in the next 2 sts, sc inc) around (16)
Round 4: (sc in the next 3 sts, sc inc) around (20)
Round 5: (sc in the next 4 sts, sc inc) around (24)
Round 6: sc in the next 3 sts, (1 hdc, 2 hdc) three times, 1 hdc, sc in the next 7 sts, (sc2tog) two times, sc in remaining 3 sts (25)
- PM in base of 1st and last hdc sts of Round 6
Round 7: (sc in ea st) around (25)
- Cc to Black
- FO with Yellow (Saffron)
Round 8: sc 6, sc 1 while attaching antenna, sc 3, sc 1 while attaching the 2nd antenna, sc 14 (25)
- Make sure the antennae are placed so they curve toward the outer sides of the head.
Round 9: (sc in ea st) around (25)
- Tie the ends of the antenna together inside of the head.
Round 10: (sc in the next 3 sts, sc2tog) around (20)
Round 11: (sc in the next 2 sts, sc2tog) around (15)
Round 12: (sc in the next st, sc2tog) around (10)

- FO with a long tail.
- Place eyes at the base of the 1st and last hdc sts (where you placed your stitch markers).
- Place cotter pin (if jointing the neck) at bottom/center between Round 7 & Round 8.
- Stuff the head.
- Use the long end for the drawstring close and use yellow (Saffron) for needle sculpting to tuck the eyes, if desired.
- Set the head aside until Round 4 of the body (if jointing the neck) or until the body is completed (if sewing the head in place).

84

HANDS and ARMS (Make 4)

- Working in continuous rounds
- Starting on the hand and working into the arm
- Working with Black yarn

Round 1: 6 sc in a magic ring (6)
Round 2 - Round 3: (sc in ea st) around (6)

- Tuck the end into the hand.
- Do not stuff.
- Pull up two more loops evenly spaced across the opening of hand; this closes the hand and provides the loops needed to start the I-cord (3 loops on hook).

I-CORD ARMS

- Working in rows
- Do NOT turn

Row 1: Drop 2 loops (pinching them so they don't unravel), ch 1, pick up 2nd loop & ch 1, pick up last loop & ch 1
Row 2 - Row 12: repeat Row 1

- To finish, yo, pull through all three, cut yarn, yo, pull through one.
- Set aside until Round 3 & Round 9 of the body.

FEET and LEGS (Make 2)

- Working in continuous rounds
- Starting on the foot and working into the leg
- Working with Black yarn

Round 1: 6 sc in a magic ring (6)
Round 2: (sc inc in ea st) around (12)
Round 3: (sc in ea st) around (12)
Round 4: (sc2tog) six times (6)

- Tuck the end into the foot.
- Do not stuff.
- Pull up two more loops evenly spaced across the opening of foot; this closes the foot and provides the loops needed to start the I-cord (3 loops on hook).

I-CORD LEGS

- Working in rows
- Do NOT turn

Row 1: Drop 2 loops (pinching them so they don't unravel), ch 1, pick up 2nd loop & ch 1, pick up last loop & ch 1
Row 2 - Row 17: repeat Row 1

- To finish, yo, pull through all three, cut yarn, yo, pull through one.
- Set aside until Round 15 of the body.

BODY

- Working from the neck down
- Working in continuous rounds
- Starting with Yellow yarn (Saffron)

Round 1: sc 6 in a magic ring (6)
Round 2: (sc inc) around (12)
Round 3: sc 3, sc 2 while joining 1st arm, sc 4, sc 2 while joining 2nd arm, sc 1 (12)
Round 4: (sc in ea st) around (12)
- Install cotter pin if jointing the neck
Round 5: (sc in ea st) around (12)
- Cc to Black
Round 6: (sc in the next 3 sts, sc inc) around (15)
Round 7: (sc in ea st) around (15)
Round 8: (sc in the next 4 sts, sc inc) around (18)
Round 9: sc 2, sc inc, sc 4, sc 2 while joining 3rd arm, sc 1, sc inc, sc 2, sc inc, sc 1, sc 2 while joining 4th arm, sc 1 (21)
- Cc to Yellow (Saffron)
Round 10 - Round 11: (sc in ea st) around (21)
Round 12: (sc in the next 6 sts, sc inc) around (24)
- Cc to Black
Round 13: (sc in the next 7 sts, sc inc) around (27)
Round 14: (sc in ea st) around (27)
Round 15: sc 14, sc 2 while joining 1st leg, sc 5, sc 2 while joining 2nd leg, sc 4 (27)
- Cc to Soft White
Round 16: (sc in the next st, sc2tog) around (18)
- Stuff the body
Round 17: repeat round 16 (12)
Round 18: (sc2tog) around (6)

- FO & drawstring close.
- Sew the head to the body if you didn't joint the neck.
- Brush or velcro the yarn to make him fuzzy, being careful not to hitch the legs.

WINGS (Make 2)

- Working with White yarn

Round 1: working all stitches into a magic ring, ch 2, 4 dc, 2 tr, ch 2, sl st in 2nd ch from the hook, 2 tr, 4 dc, join in top of 1st dc st

- FO with long ends.
- Sew to the body, level with the 1st set of arms.

Using the hooked side of a large piece of velcro

Press onto crochet, then pull/drag over the surface

Protect the limbs with your hand

Continue until fuzzy

Floppy Flamingo

MATERIALS:

- Worsted weight yarn (medium 4)
    - Red Heart Super Saver in Flamingo (37 g)
    - Red Heart Super Saver in Baby Pink (2.5 g)
    - Red Heart Super Saver in Aran (1.5 g)
    - Red Heart Super Saver in Black (1 g)
- 4 mm hook
- Stitch marker(s)
- Scissors
- Fiberfill
- 12 mm safety eyes in yellow
- Doll-making needle
- Optional: one 3/32″ x 1 ½″ cotter pin, one 3/32″ x 3/16″ hitch pin clip, two 3/16″ fender washers, two No. 6 countersunk finishing washers, and pliers for bending the cotter pin (if you are doing the jointed neck)

ABBREVIATIONS USED IN THIS FLOPPY:

BLO - Back Loop Only
Cc - Color Change
Ch - Chain
Dc - Double Crochet
Ea - Each
FLO - Front Loop Only

FO - Finish Off
Hdc - Half Double Crochet
Inc - Increase
PM - Place Marker
Sc - Single Crochet
Sc2tog - Single Crochet Two Together

Sl st - Slip Stitch
St(s) - Stitch or Stitches
Tr - Treble
Yo - Yarn Over

Floppy Flamingo Teaches:

- Working in available Front Loops - pg. 160
- Tacking to hook the bill - pg. 90

HEAD

- Working from the beak to the back of the head
- Starting with Black yarn
- Working in continuous rounds

Round 1: sc 4 in a magic ring (4)
Round 2 - Round 3: (sc in ea st) around (4)
Round 4: (sc in the next st, sc inc) around (6)
- Sl st in next st and FO
- Cc to Aran
- Join with sc in any stitch

Round 5: (sc in ea st) around (6)
Round 6: (sc in the next 2 sts, sc inc) around (8)
Round 7 - Round 8: (sc in ea st) around (8)
Round 9: (sc in the next st, sc inc) around (12)
Round 10: (sc in ea st) around (12)
Round 11: (sc in the next 2 sts, sc inc) around (16)
- Sl st into next st and FO
- Cc to main color (Flamingo)
- Join with sc in any stitch

Round 12: (sc in the next 3 sts, sc inc) around (20)
Round 13: (sc in the next 4 sts, sc inc) around (24)
Round 14: sc in the next 3 sts, (1 hdc, 2 hdc) three times, 1 hdc, sc in the next 7 sts, (sc2tog) two times, sc in remaining 3 sts (25)
- PM in base of 1st and last hdc sts of Round 14

Round 15 - Round 17: (sc in ea st) around (25)
Round 18: (sc in the next 3 sts, sc2tog) around (20)
Round 19: (sc in the next 2 sts, sc2tog) around (15)
Round 20: (sc in the next st, sc2tog) around (10)

- FO with a long tail.
- Place eyes at the base of the 1st and last hdc sts (where you placed your stitch markers).
- Place cotter pin (if jointing the neck) at bottom/center between Round 15 & Round 16.
- Stuff the head, lightly stuffing the beak area.
- Use the long end for the drawstring close and for needle sculpting to tuck the eyes, if desired.
- Set the head aside until Round 4 of the body (if jointing the neck) or until the body is completed (if sewing the head in place).

Through the head and out at the front of the bill

One stitch over and back through the head...

Coming out through the same stitch

Pull the ends to create the hook in the bill

Tie off and hide the ends inside the head

LARGE FEATHER
(Make 2)

- Working in continuous rounds
- Working with Pink yarn (Flamingo)

Round 1: sc 6 into a magic ring (6)
Round 2: (sc inc) around (12)
Round 3 - Round 5: (sc in ea st) around (12)
Round 6: (sc2tog, sc 4) twice (10)
Round 7: (sc in ea st) around (10)
Round 8: (sc2tog, sc 3) twice (8)
Round 9: (sc in ea st) around (8)
Round 10: (sc2tog, sc2) twice (6)

- FO and set aside until the last feather is complete.

MIDDLE FEATHER
(Make 2)

- Working in continuous rounds
- Working with Pink yarn (Flamingo)

Round 1: sc 5 into a magic ring (5)
Round 2: (sc inc) around (10)
Round 3 - Round 5: (sc in ea st) around (10)
Round 6: (sc2tog, sc 3) twice (8)
Round 7: (sc2tog, sc 2) twice (6)
Round 8: (sc in ea st) around (6)

- FO and set aside until the last feather is complete.

SMALL FEATHER
(Make 2)

- Working in continuous rounds
- Working with Pink yarn (Flamingo)

Round 1: sc 4 into a magic ring (4)
Round 2: (sc inc) around (8)
Round 3 - Round 5: (sc in ea st) around (8)
Round 6: (sc2tog, sc 2) twice (6)

- Do NOT FO
- Continue to "Putting Feathers Together and Forming the Wings."

PUTTING FEATHERS TOGETHER AND FORMING THE WINGS (Make 2)

- With the smallest feather still on the hook, and using its working yarn
- Hiding the ends inside as you go
- Do NOT stuff

Round 1: sc in next 3 sts of small feather, sc in 3 sc sts of middle feather, sc in all 6 sc sts of large feather, moving back along the other side of the feathers, sc in 3 sc sts of the middle feather, sc in the 3 remaining sts of the first feather (18)
Round 2: (BLO sc in ea st) aorund (18)
Round 3: (sc 4, sc2tog) around (15)
Round 4: (sc 3, sc2tog) around (12)
Round 5: sc 6 to close (6)

- FO with a long tail to use for sewing to the body.
- Set aside until the body is completed.

FEET (Make 2)

- Starting with a long tail to use for darning
- Working with Dark Pink yarn (Flamingo)

Row 1: ch 4, working in the back bumps of ch, sl st in closest ch to hook, sl st in the next ch, sc in ea of the last 2 chains (1st toe complete)

Row 2: ch 1, turn, sc in ea of the next 2 sc, ch 3, working in the back bumps of ch, sl st in closest ch to hook, sl st in next 2 chains, sc in the next 2 sc (2nd toe complete)

Row 3: ch 1, turn, sc in the next 2 sc, ch 2, working in the back bumps of the ch, sl st in the closest ch to the hook, sl st in the next ch, sc in the next 2 sc (3rd toe complete)

Row 4: Working across the top of the ankle, insert hook, yo, pull up loop under middle toe, insert hook in corner st, yo, pull up loop (3 loops on hook)

- Use the 3 loops on the hook to begin the I-cord.
- Do NOT finish off.
- Use the working yarn to move on to the legs.

I-CORD LEGS (Make 2)

- Beginning with the 3 loops on the hook

Row 1: Drop 2 loops (pinching them so they don't unravel), ch 1, pick up 2nd loop & ch 1, pick up last loop & ch 1

Row 2 - Row 20: repeat Row 1

- To finish, yo, pull through all three, yo, pull through one.
- Use the end at the ankle to darn into the foot.
- Set aside until Round 25 of the body.

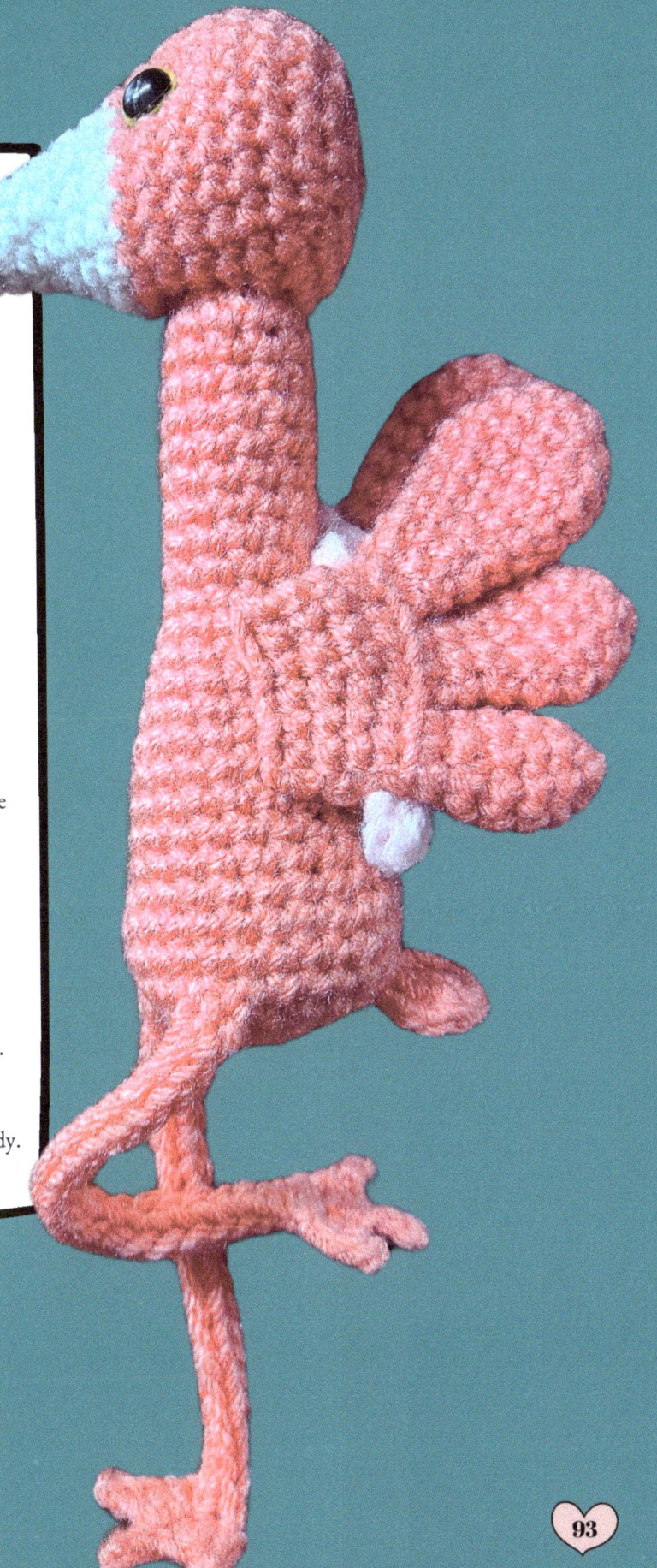

BODY

- Working from the neck down
- Working in continuous rounds
- Working with Pink yarn (Flamingo)

Round 1: sc 6 in a magic ring (6)
Round 2: (sc inc) around (12)
Round 3 - Round 4: (sc in ea st) around (12)
- Install cotter pin if jointing the neck
- Stuff the neck as you go
Round 5 - Round 13: (sc in ea st) around (12)
Round 14: (sc in the next 3 sts, sc inc) around (15)
Round 15 - Round 16: (sc in ea st) around (15)
Round 17: (sc in the next 4 sts, sc inc) around (18)
Round 18: (sc in the next 5 sts, sc inc) around (21)
Round 19 - Round 21: (sc in ea st) around (21)
Round 22: (sc in the next 6 sts, sc inc) around (24)
Round 23: (sc in the next 7 sts, sc inc) around (27)
Round 24: (sc in ea st) around (27)
Round 25: sc 12, sc 2 while joining 1st leg, sc 5, sc 2 while joining the 2nd leg, sc 6 (27)
Round 26: (sc in the next st, sc2tog) around (18)
- Stuff the body
Round 27: repeat round 26 (12)
Round 28: (sc2tog) around (6)

- FO & drawstring close.
- Sew the head to the body if you didn't joint the neck.
- Sew the wings in place at Flamingo's sides, between Rounds 14 & 19.
- Darn or hide any remaining loose ends inside the body.
- Add scallops to the back of the wings.

SCALLOPS

- Using available FLO on the top side of the wings
- Working with hook pointing towards the wing tips
- Working with Light Pink yarn (Baby Pink)

Row 1: Join with a sc, (dc 3 in the next st, sc in the next) repeat three more times (4 scallops)

- FO and hide the ends inside.
- Set aside until the body is complete.

TAIL

- Working with Pink yarn (Flamingo)
- Rooting the tail directly to the body on same round as legs (Round 25)
- Rooting the tail over the 3 center/back stitches of the bum
- Inserting the hook pointing downwards

Row 1: join with a sl st, ch 2, tr 2 times in the same st, tr 3 in next st, tr 2 in 3rd st, ch 2, sl st in same st

- FO.
- Hide the ends inside the body.

Floppy Butterfly

MATERIALS:

- Worsted weight yarn (medium 4)
  - Red Heart Super Saver in Charcoal (32 g)
  - Red Heart Super Saver in Blue (16.5 g)
  - Red Heart Super Saver in Light Blue (16.5 g)
- 4 mm hook
- Stitch marker(s)
- Scissors
- Fiberfill
- 12 mm safety eyes in blue
- Doll-making needle
- Optional: Sewer's Chalk
- Optional: one 3/32" x 1 ½" cotter pin, one 3/32" x 3/16" hitch pin clip, two 3/16" fender washers, two No. 6 countersunk finishing washers, and pliers for bending the cotter pin (if you are doing the jointed neck)

ABBREVIATIONS USED IN THIS FLOPPY:

BLO - Back Loop Only
Ch - Chain
Ea - Each
FO - Finish Off
Hdc - Half Double Crochet

Inc - Increase
PM - Place Marker
Sc - Single Crochet
Sc2tog - Single Crochet Two Together
Sk - Skip

Sl st - Slip Stitch
St(s) - Stitch or Stitches
Yo - Yarn Over

Floppy Butterfly Teaches:

- Joining panels with single crochet stitches – pg. 102

ANTENNA (Make 2)

Special Stitch Instructions for Puff Stitch:
Yo, insert in back bump of the 2nd ch from hook, yo, pull up loop, yo, insert hook into same st, yo, pull up loop, yo, pull through all 5 loops on the hook.

- With Dark Grey yarn (Charcoal)
- Starting and finishing with a long tail for tying off inside of the head

Row 1: ch 7
Row 2: puff st in the 2nd ch from the hook, sl st in the same st, sc 6 AROUND the ch, sc in the back bump of the last ch st.

- FO.
- Set aside until Round 9 of the head.

HEAD

- Working from the nose to back of the head
- Working in continuous rounds
- Working with Dark Grey yarn (Charcoal)

Round 1: sc 6 into a magic ring (6)
Round 2: (sc inc in ea st) around (12)
Round 3: (sc in the next 2 sts, sc inc) around (16)
Round 4: (sc in the next 3 sts, sc inc) around (20)
Round 5: (sc in the next 4 sts, sc inc) around (24)
Round 6: sc in the next 3 sts, (1 hdc, 2 hdc) three times, 1 hdc, sc in the next 7 sts, (sc2tog) two times, sc in remaining 3 sts (25)
- PM in base of 1st and last hdc sts of Round 6
Round 7: (sc in ea st) around (25)
Round 8: sc 6, sc 1 while attaching antenna, sc 3, sc 1 while attaching the 2nd antenna, sc 14 (25)
- Make sure the antennae are placed so they curve toward the outer sides of the head.
Round 9: (sc in ea st) around (25)
- Tie the ends of the antenna together inside of the head
Round 10: (sc in the next 3 sts, sc2tog) around (20)
Round 11: (sc in the next 2 sts, sc2tog) around (15)
Round 12: (sc in the next st, sc2tog) around (10)

- FO with a long tail.
- Place eyes at the base of the 1st and last hdc sts (where you placed your stitch markers).
- Place cotter pin (if jointing the neck) at bottom/center between Round 7 & Round 8.
- Stuff the head.
- Use the long end for the drawstring close and for needle sculpting to tuck the eyes, if desired.
- Set the head aside until Round 4 of the body (if jointing the neck) or until the body is completed (if sewing the head in place).

HANDS and ARMS (Make 4)

- Working in continuous rounds
- Starting with the hand and working into the arm
- Working with Dark Grey yarn (Charcoal)

Round 1: 6 sc in a magic ring (6)
Round 2 - Round 3: (sc in ea st) around (6)

- Tuck the end into the hand.
- Do not stuff.
- Pull up two more loops evenly spaced across the opening of the hand; this closes the hand and provides the loops needed to start the I-cord (3 loops on hook).

I-CORD ARMS

- Working in rows
- Do NOT turn

Row 1: Drop 2 loops (pinching them so they don't unravel), ch 1, pick up 2nd loop & ch 1, pick up last loop & ch 1
Row 2 - Row 12: repeat Row 1

- To finish, yo, pull through all three, cut yarn, yo, pull through one.
- Set aside until Round 3 & Round 9 of the body.

FEET and LEGS (Make 2)

- Working in continuous rounds
- Starting with the foot and working into the leg
- Working with Dark Grey yarn (Charcoal)

Round 1: 6 sc in a magic ring (6)
Round 2: (sc inc in ea st) around (12)
Round 3: (sc in ea st) around (12)
Round 4: (sc2tog) six times (6)

- Tuck the end into the foot.
- Do not stuff.
- Pull up two more loops evenly spaced across the opening of the foot; this closes the foot and provides the loops needed to start the I-cord (3 loops on hook).

I-CORD LEGS

- Working in rows
- Do NOT turn

Row 1: Drop 2 loops (pinching them so they don't unravel), ch 1, pick up 2nd loop & ch 1, pick up last loop & ch 1
Row 2 - Row 17: repeat Row 1

- To finish, yo, pull through all three, cut yarn, yo, pull through one.
- Set aside until Round 15 of the body.

BODY

- Working from the neck down
- Working in continuous rounds
- Working with Dark Grey yarn (Charcoal)

Round 1: sc 6 in a magic ring (6)
Round 2: (sc inc) around (12)
Round 3: sc 3, sc 2 while joining 1st arm, sc 4, sc 2 while joining 2nd arm, sc 1 (12)
Round 4: (sc in ea st) around (12)
- Install cotter pin if jointing the neck
Round 5: (sc in ea st) around (12)
Round 6: (sc in the next 3 sts, sc inc) around (15)
Round 7: (sc in ea st) around (15)
Round 8: (sc in the next 4 sts, sc inc) around (18)
Round 9: sc 2, sc inc, sc 4, sc 2 while joining 3rd arm, sc 1, sc inc, sc 2, sc inc, sc 1, sc 2 while joining 4th arm, sc 1 (21)
Round 10 - Round 11: (sc in ea st) around (21)
Round 12: (sc in the next 6 sts, sc inc) around (24)
Round 13: (sc in the next 7 sts, sc inc) around (27)
Round 14: (sc in ea st) around (27)
Round 15: sc 14, sc 2 while joining 1st leg, sc 5, sc 2 while joining 2nd leg, sc 4 (27)
Round 16: (sc in the next st, sc2tog) around (18)
- Stuff the body
Round 17: repeat round 16 (12)
Round 18: (sc2tog) around (6)

- FO & drawstring close.
- Sew the head to the body if you didn't joint the neck.

100

LARGE WING PANELS (Make 2 in lighter color and 2 in darker color)

- Working in rows
- Ch 1 to turn, does not count as a stitch
- Colors shown are Blue and Light Blue in Red Heart Super Saver

Row 1: ch 22 (22)
Row 2: turn, working in the back bumps of the ch, sk 1, sl st, sc, hdc 2 in next st, hdc in the next 15 sts, sc in the next 3 sts (22)

- Working in BLO on every stitch for the rest of the wing

Row 3: ch 1, turn, sc in the next 3 sts, hdc in the next 14 sts, sc in the next st, sl st in the next st, leave remaining sts unworked (19)
Row 4: ch 1, turn, sk 1, sc, hdc in the next 14 sts, sc in the remaining 3 sts (18)
Row 5: ch 1, turn, sc in the next 3 sts, hdc in the next 11 sts, sc, sl st, leave remaining sts unworked (16)
Row 6: ch 1, turn, sk 1, sc, hdc in the next 11 sts, sc in the remaining 3 sts (15)
Row 7: ch 1, turn, sc in the next 3 sts, hdc in the next 8 sts, sc, sl st, leave remaining sts unworked (13)
Row 8: ch 1, turn, sk 1, sc, hdc in the next 8 sts, sc in the remaining 3 sts (12)
Row 9: Place 4 sc sts evenly spaced up the inside edge of the wing. Place one in ea turning ch, and one in the corner at the beginning of the original starting ch (4)

- FO and set aside until all wing parts have been made.

SMALL WING PANELS (Make 2 in lighter color and 2 in darker color)

- Working in rows
- Ch 1 to turn, does not count as a stitch
- Colors shown are Blue and Light Blue in Red Heart Super Saver

Row 1: ch 15 (15)
Row 2: turn, working in the back bumps of the ch, sk 1, sl st, sc, hdc 2 in next st, hdc in the next 8 sts, sc in the next 3 sts (15)

- Working in BLO on every stitch for the rest of the wing

Row 3: ch 1, turn, sc in the next 3 sts, hdc in the next 7 sts, sc in the next st, sl st in the next st, leave remaining sts unworked (12)
Row 4: ch 1, turn, sk 1, sc, hdc in the next 7 sts, sc in the remaining 3 sts (11)
Row 5: ch 1, turn, sc in the next 3 sts, hdc in the next 4 sts, sc, sl st, leave remaining sts unworked (9)
Row 6: ch 1, turn, sk 1, sc, hdc in the next 4 sts, sc in the remaining 3 sts (8)
Row 7: Place 3 sc sts evenly spaced up the inside edge of the wing. Place one in ea turning ch, and one in the corner at the beginning of the original starting ch (3)

- FO and set aside until all wing parts have been made, then continue to Wing Edging.

WING EDGING

- Crocheting the front and back panels of each wing together with sc sts
- Joining in the first available st along the top starting chains of the wings
- When working on opposite wings, be sure to reverse the colors.
- Hiding the ends between the wings
- Working with Dark Grey yarn (Charcoal)

Working around the edge of the large wing panels:

Start in the side st and sc across the starting ch

Across the top- join with a sc st in the top corner/side st, sc 20 across the starting ch, sc 3 in last st at the wing's tip (24)

Down the outer edge- sc outer edge of wing panels together with 14 evenly spaced sts (14)

Across the bottom- sc the bottom edges of the wing panels together with 11 sc sts (11)

Up the inside edge- sc 3 up the inside edge, in the last st at the top inside corner of the wing sc 2, sl st in 1st st of edging (6)

Working around the edge of the small wing panels:

Across the top- join with a sc st in the top corner/side st, sc 13 across the starting ch, sc 3 in last st at the wing's tip (17)

Down the outer edge- sc outer edge of wing panels together with 10 evenly spaced sts (10)

Across the bottom- sc the bottom edges of the wing panels together with 7 sc sts (7)

Up the inside edge- sc 2 up the inside edge, in the last st at the top inside corner of the wing sc 2, sl st in 1st st of edging (5)

JOINING WINGS

- Postion the wings with the outer corners pointing upward and all like colors facing the same side.
- Working with Dark Grey yarn (Charcoal)

Sc together top wings with 5 sts, lay bottom wings on the outside and sc 2 through all four wings, sc 3 through each bottom wing

- FO with a long tail to sew to the back.
- Tip: draw a line down the center of the back with sewer's chalk and follow it to sew the wings on straight.

Working down the center join the top wings

To join the samller wings work through all 4 wings

Join with like colors facing the same direction

Finish by joining the edge of the bottom two wings

View of the under side of the wings

View of the top side of the wings

Floppy Frog

MATERIALS:

- Worsted weight yarn (medium 4)
  - Red Heart Super Saver in Tea Leaf (19.5 g)
  - Red Heart Super Saver in White (1 g)
- 4 mm hook
- Stitch marker(s)
- Scissors
- Fiberfill
- 12 mm safety cat eyes in green
- Doll-making needle
- Optional: one 3/32" x 1 ½" cotter pin, one 3/32" x 3/16" hitch pin clip, two 3/16" fender washers, two No. 6 countersunk finishing washers, and pliers for bending the cotter pin (if you are doing the jointed neck)

ABBREVIATIONS USED IN THIS FLOPPY:

Ch - Chain	Sc - Single Crochet	Yo - Yarn Over
Ea - Each	Sc2tog - Single Crochet Two Together	
FO - Finish Off	Sc3tog - Single Crochet Three Together	
Hdc - Half Double Crochet	Sl st - Slip Stitch	
Inc - Increase	St(s) - Stitch or Stitches	

Floppy Frog Teaches:

- Sc3tog - pg. 149
- Working in the 3rd loop - pg. 147

EYE WHITES (Make 2)

- Working with White yarn
- Ch 1 does not count as a stitch

Round 1: sc 6 in a magic ring, join with sl st (6)
- Do not cinch the magic ring down too tightly as we will want room to place the safety eyes later

Round 2: ch 1, do NOT turn, sc 1 in same st as join, (sc inc) four times, sc (10)

- FO.
- Set aside until Round 7 of the head.

HEAD

- Working from the nose to the back of the head
- Working in continuous rounds
- Working with Green yarn (Tea Leaf)

Round 1: 4 sc in a magic ring (4)
Round 2: (sc inc in each st) around (8)
Round 3: (sc in the next st, sc inc) around (12)
Round 4: (sc in the next 2 sts, sc inc) around (16)
Round 5: (sc in the next 3 sts, sc inc) around (20)
Round 6: (sc in the next 4 sts, sc inc) around (24)
Round 7: sc 2, attach along bottom of 1st eye white with 4 sc sts, sc, attach along bottom of 2nd eye white with 4 sc sts, sc 6, (sc2tog) twice, sc 3 (22)
Round 8: sc 2, sc in the corner of the eye, hdc 9 over the 1st eye white, sl st in between the eyes, hdc 9 over the 2nd eye white, sc in the corner of the eye white, sc 11 (34)
Round 9: sc, sc2tog, sc 8 in 3rd loop, sc2tog in the 3rd loop while skipping the sl st from the previous round, sc 8 in 3rd loop, sc2tog, sc 10 (30)
Round 10: (sc2tog) twice, (sc inc) four times, sc, sc3tog, sc, (sc inc) four times, (sc2tog) twice, sc 9 (32)
Round 11: sc2tog, sc 6, (sc2tog) four times, sc 6, sc2tog, sc 8 (26)
Round 12: (sc2tog) eight times, sc 10 (18)
Round 13: (sc2tog) around (9)

- FO with a long tail.
- Place eyes in the center of the magic rings of the eye whites.
- Place cotter pin (if jointing the neck) at bottom/center between Round 8 & Round 9.
- Stuff the head.
- Use the long end for the drawstring close and for needle sculpting, and white yarn to tuck the eyes, if desired.
- Set the head aside until Round 4 of the body (if jointing the neck) or until the body is completed (if sewing the head in place).

HANDS and FEET (Make 4)

Special Stitch Instructions for Puff Stitch: Yo, insert in 2nd ch from the hook, yo, pull up loop (3 loops on hook), yo, insert in same st, yo, pull up loop (5 loops on hook), yo, pull through all.

- Starting with a long tail to use for darning
- Working with Green yarn (Tea Leaf)
- Working in the back bumps of the chain stitches throughout

Row 1: ch 5, puff st, sl st in the same st, sl st in the next ch, sc in ea of the last 2 chains
Row 2: ch 1, turn, sc in ea of the next 2 sc, ch 4, puff st, sl st in same st, sl st in next 2 chains, sc in ea of the next 2 sc
Row 3: ch 1, turn, sc in ea of the next 2 sc, ch 3, puff st, sl st in the same st, sl st in the next ch, sc in ea of the next 2 sc
Row 4: Working across the top of the hand/foot insert hook, yo, and pull up loop under middle finger, insert hook in corner st, yo, pull up loop (3 loops on hook)

- Use the 3 loops on hook to begin the I-cord.
- Do NOT finish off.
- Use the working yarn to move on to the arms and legs.

I-CORD ARMS (Make 2)

- Beginning with 3 loops on hook

Row 1: Drop 2 loops (pinching them so they don't unravel), ch 1, pick up 2nd loop & ch 1, pick up last loop & ch 1
Row 2 - Row 11: repeat Row 1

- To finish, yo, pull through all three, yo, pull through one.
- Use the end at the wrist to darn into the hand.
- Set aside until Round 3 of the body.

I-CORD LEGS (Make 2)

- Beginning with 3 loops on hook

Row 1: Drop 2 loops (pinching them so they don't unravel), ch 1, pick up 2nd loop & ch 1, pick up last loop & ch 1
Row 2 - Row 17: repeat Row 1

- To finish, yo, pull through all three, yo, pull through one.
- Use the end at the ankle to darn into the foot.
- Set aside until Round 15 of the body.

BODY

- Working from the neck down
- Working in continuous rounds
- Working with Green yarn (Tea Leaf)

Round 1: sc 6 in a magic ring (6)
Round 2: (sc inc) around (12)
Round 3: sc 3, sc 2 while joining 1st arm, sc 4, sc 2 while joining 2nd arm, sc 1 (12)
Round 4: (sc in ea st) around (12)
- Install cotter pin if jointing the neck
Round 5: (sc in ea st) around (12)
Round 6: (sc in the next 3 sts, sc inc) around (15)
Round 7: (sc in ea st) around (15)
Round 8: (sc in the next 4 sts, sc inc) around (18)
Round 9: (sc in the next 5 sts, sc inc) around (21)
Round 10 - Round 11: (sc in ea st) around (21)
Round 12: (sc in the next 6 sts, sc inc) around (24)
Round 13: (sc in the next 7 sts, sc inc) around (27)
Round 14: (sc in ea st) around (27)
Round 15: sc 14, sc 2 while joining 1st leg, sc 5, sc 2 while joining 2nd leg, sc 4 (27)
Round 16: (sc in the next st, sc2tog) around (18)
- Stuff the body
Round 17: repeat round 16 (12)
Round 18: (sc2tog) around (6)

- FO & drawstring close.
- Sew the head to the body if you didn't joint the neck.

Floppy Bird

MATERIALS:

- Worsted weight yarn (medium 4)
  - Red Heart Super Saver in Turqua (33.5 g)
  - Red Heart Super Saver in Charcoal (4.5 g)
- 4 mm hook
- Stitch marker(s)
- Scissors
- Fiberfill
- 12 mm safety eyes in brown
- Doll-making needle
- Optional: one 3/32" x 1 ½" cotter pin, one 3/32" x 3/16" hitch pin clip, two 3/16" fender washers, two No. 6 countersunk finishing washers, and pliers for bending the cotter pin (if you are doing the jointed neck)

ABBREVIATIONS USED IN THIS FLOPPY:

BLO - Back Loop Only
Ch - Chain
Dc - Double Crochet
Ea - Each
FO - Finish Off

Hdc - Half Double Crochet
Inc - Increase
PM - Place Marker
Sc - Single Crochet
Sc2tog - Single Crochet Two Together

Sk - Skip
Sl st - Slip Stitch
St(s) - Stitch or Stitches
Yo - Yarn Over

Floppy Bird Teaches:

Tunisian Simple Stitch - pg. 114

HEAD

- Working from the front to back of the head
- Working with Blue yarn (Turqua)

Round 1: sc 6 into a magic ring (6)
Round 2: (sc inc in ea st) around (12)
Round 3: (sc in the next 2 sts, sc inc) around (16)
Round 4: (sc in the next 3 sts, sc inc) around (20)
Round 5: (sc in the next 4 sts, sc inc) around (24)
Round 6: sc in the next 3 sts, (1 hdc, 2 hdc) three times, 1 hdc, sc in the next 7 sts, (sc2tog) two times, sc in remaining 3 sts (25)
- PM in base of 1st and last hdc sts of Round 6
Round 7 - Round 9: (sc in ea st) around (25)
Round 10: (sc in the next 3 sts, sc2tog) around (20)
Round 11: (sc in the next 2 sts, sc2tog) around (15)
Round 12: (sc in the next st, sc2tog) around (10)

- FO with a long tail.
- Place eyes at the base of the 1st and last hdc sts (where you placed your stitch markers).
- Place cotter pin (if jointing the neck) at bottom/center between Round 7 & Round 8.
- Stuff the head.
- Use the long end for the drawstring close and for needle sculpting to tuck the eyes, if desired.
- Set the head aside until Round 4 of the body (if jointing the neck) or until the body is completed (if sewing the head in place).

BEAK

- Working with Dark Grey yarn (Charcoal)
- Root with the hook pointing towards the top of the head in 2nd round of the face
- Working in the 3 center sts above the magic circle

In First Stitch- Sc, dc
In Middle Stitch- dc, ch 2, sl st in 2nd from hook, dc
In Third Stitch- dc, sc
To Form Lower Beak- ch 3, sl st in 2nd ch from hook, hdc in rem ch st, sl st in the top of the beginning sc st

- FO.
- Stitch the bottom edge of the lower bill to the face.
- Tie off and hide the ends.

Rooting through the stitches of the face

Complete the top beak over 3 sts of the face

Make the bottom beak...

Pull it into place with a sl st in the 1st st of the top beak

FEET (Make 2)

- Working with Charcoal yarn
- Starting with a long tail for darning

Row 1: ch 4, working in the back bumps of ch, sl st in closest ch to hook, sl st in the next 2 ch, sc in the last ch

Row 2: ch 1, turn, sc in the next sc, ch 4, working in the back bumps of ch, sl st in closest ch to hook, sl st in next 3 chains, sc in sc st (mark this st), ch 3, sl st in the closest ch to the hook, sl st in next 2 chains (this forms the back toe), sl st in the sc on the other side of the middle toe (between the first & the second toe), ch 1, bring ch over the back toe just made and sc in the sc st on the other side of the middle toe in the marked st (place new marker)

Row 3: ch 3, working in the back bumps of the ch, sl st in the closest ch to the hook, sl st in the next 2 ch, sc in the last sc st from Round 2 (the marked st)

Row 4: Working across the top of the foot, insert hook, yo, pull up loop above the middle and back (fold the back toe against the bottom of the foot to do this), insert hook in corner st, yo, pull up loop (3 loops on hook)

- Do NOT FO.
- Use the 3 loops on the hook to begin the I-cord.

For back toe, place marker at the end of the 2nd toe

Crochet back toe, then sl st between 1st and middle toe

Ch 1

Reaching back to the stitch with the marker, place a sc st

Place new marker and complete the last toe

Pick up the sts for the I-cord across the top of the foot

I-CORD LEGS (Make 2)

- Beginning with 3 loops on the hook

Row 1: Drop 2 loops (pinching them so they don't unravel), ch 1, pick up 2nd loop & ch 1, pick up last loop & ch 1

Row 2 - Row 17: repeat Row 1

- To finish, yo, pull through all three, yo, pull through one.
- Use the end at the ankle to darn into the foot.
- Set aside until Round 15 of the body.

TAIL FEATHER (Make 1)

- Working in main color (Turqua)
- Working tunisian simple stitch on both sides of a starting ch

Row 1: ch 16 (16)
Row 2: starting in the 2nd ch from the hook, pick up a loop in ea st across (16 loops on the hook)
Row 3: working the loops off the hook, yo, pull through 1, (yo, pull through 2) fifteen times, ch 3, sc through 3rd ch from hook
Row 4: working through the other side of the staring ch, pick up 15 loops (16 loops on the hook)
Row 5: working the loops off the hook, yo, pull through 1, (yo, pull through 2) thirteen times, yo, pull through remaining 3 loops on the hook

- FO.
- Darn ends.

TAIL FEATHERS (Make 2)

- Working in main color (Turqua)
- Working tunisian simple stitch on both sides of a starting ch

Row 1: ch 11 (11)
Row 2: starting in the 2nd ch from the hook, pick up a loop in ea st across (11 loops on the hook)
Row 3: working the loops off the hook, yo, pull through 1, (yo, pull through 2) ten times, ch 3, sc through 3rd ch from hook
Row 4: working through the other side of the staring ch, pick up 10 loops (11 loops on the hook)
Row 5: working the loops off the hook, yo, pull through 1, (yo, pull through 2) eight times, yo, pull through remaining 3 loops on the hook

- FO.
- Darn ends.

Pick up a st through each chain

Work the loops off the hook and create the point

Pick up the stitches down the other side of the chain

Work the loop off the hook and FO

JOINING THE TAIL FEATHERS

- Working in main color (Turqua)

Row 1-
- Using 4 sc to join, as follows...

Work the 1st sc in the 1st half of the top of short feather

Work the 2nd sc through the top of the middle (longest) feather and the other half of the top of the 1st feather

Work the 3rd sc through the other half of the middle feather and the 1st half of the last feather

Work the 4th sc through the other top half of the last feather

Row 2: ch 1, turn, (sc in ea st) across (4)

- Set aside until Round 15 of the body.

Place sc sts at the top end of the feathers...

then working through both feathers at the same time

Attach with four sc sts total across the top

Work one more row of sc sts across the top

WINGS (Make 2)

- Working in rows
- Ch 1 to turn, does not count as a stitch
- Working with Blue yarn (Turqua)

Row 1: ch 22 (22)
Row 2: turn, working in the back bumps of the ch, sk 1, sl st, sc, hdc 2 in next st, hdc in the next 15 sts, sc in the next 3 sts (22)

- Working in BLO on every stitch for the rest of the wing

Row 3: ch 1, turn, sc in the next 3 sts, hdc in the next 14 sts, sc in the next st, sl st in the next st (19)
Row 4: ch 1, turn, sk 1, sc, hdc in the next 14 sts, sc in the remaining 3 sts (18)
Row 5: ch 1, turn, sc in the next 3 sts, hdc in the next 11 sts, sc, sl st (16)
Row 6: ch 1, turn, sk 1, sc, hdc in the next 11 sts, sc in the remaining 3 sts (15)
Row 7: ch 1, turn, sc in the next 3 sts, hdc in the next 8 sts, sc, sl st (13)
Row 8: ch 1, turn, sk 1, sc, hdc in the next 8 sts, sc in the remaining 3 sts (12)
Row 9: to pull in the pleats of the wing, place 4 sc sts evenly spaced up the inside edge of the wing. Place one in ea turning ch, and one in the corner at the beginning of the original starting ch (4)

- FO and set aside until Round 3 of the body.

BODY

- Working from the neck down to the bottom
- Working in continuous rounds
- Working with Blue yarn (Turqua)

Round 1: sc 6 in a magic ring (6)
Round 2: (sc inc) around (12)
Round 3: sc in next st, sc 3 while joining the 1st wing, sc 5, sc 3 while joining 2nd wing (12)
Round 4: (sc in ea st) around (12)

- Install cotter pin if jointing the neck

Round 5: (sc in ea st) around (12)
Round 6: (sc in the next 3 sts, sc inc) around (15)
Round 7: (sc in ea st) around (15)
Round 8: (sc in the next 4 sts, sc inc) around (18)
Round 9: (sc in the next 5 sts, sc inc) around (21)
Round 10 - Round 11: (sc in ea st) around (21)
Round 12: (sc in the next 6 sts, sc inc) around (24)
Round 13: (sc in the next 7 sts, sc inc) around (27)
Round 14: (sc in ea st) around (27)
Round 15: sc in next st, sc 4 while joining the tail, sc 7, sc 2 while joining 1st leg, sc 5, sc 2 while joining the 2nd leg, sc 6 (27)
Round 16: (sc in the next st, sc2tog) around (18)

- Stuff the body

Round 17: repeat round 16 (12)
Round 18: (sc2tog) around (6)

- FO & drawstring close.
- Sew the head to the body if you didn't joint the neck.
- Darn or hide any remaining loose ends inside the body.

Attaching wings- View from working side

Top view

Floppy Tortoise

MATERIALS:

- Worsted weight yarn (medium 4)
  - Red Heart Super Saver in Tea Leaf (27.5 g)
  - Red Heart Super Saver in Lemon (14.5 g)
  - Red Heart Super Saver in Aran for the claws (2.5 g)
- 4 mm hook
- Stitch marker(s)
- Scissors
- Fiberfill
- 12 mm safety eyes in brown
- Doll-making needle
- Optional: one 3/32" x 1 ½" cotter pin, one 3/32" x 3/16" hitch pin clip, two 3/16" fender washers, two No. 6 countersunk finishing washers, and pliers for bending the cotter pin (if you are doing the jointed neck)

ABBREVIATIONS USED IN THIS FLOPPY:

BLO - Back Loop Only
Cc - Color Change
Ch - Chain
Dc - Double Crochet
Ea - Each
FLO - Front Loop Only

FO - Finish Off
Fpdc - Front Post Double Crochet
Hdc - Half Double Crochet
Inc - Increase
PM - Place Marker
Sc - Single Crochet

Sc2tog - Single Crochet Two Together
Sl st - Slip Stitch
Slst2tog - Slip Stitch Two Together
St(s) - Stitch or Stitches
Yo - Yarn Over

Floppy Tortoise Teaches:

- Front post double crochet - pg. 122
- slst2tog - pg. 124
- Invisible join - pg. 154
- Right & Wrong side - pg. 146

HEAD

- Working from the nose to the back of the head
- Working in continuous rounds
- Working with Green yarn (Tea Leaf)

Round 1: sc 4 in a magic ring (4)
Round 2: (sc inc each st) around (8)
Round 3: (sc in the next st, sc inc) around (12)
Round 4: (sc in the next 2 sts, sc inc) around (16)
Round 5: (sc in the next 3 sts, sc inc) around (20)
Round 6: (sc in the next 4 sts, sc inc) around (24)
Round 7: sc in the next 3 sts, (1 hdc, hdc inc) three times, 1 hdc, sc in the next 7 sts, (sc2tog) two times, sc in remaining 3 sts (25)
- PM in base of 1st and last hdc sts of Round 7

Round 8 - Round 10: (sc in ea st) around (25)
Round 11: (sc in the next 3 sts, sc2tog) around (20)
Round 12: (sc in the next 2 sts, sc2tog) around (15)
Round 13: (sc in the next st, sc2tog) around (10)

- FO with a long tail.
- Place eyes at the base of the 1st and last hdc sts (where you placed your stitch markers).
- Place cotter pin (if jointing the neck) at bottom/center between Round 7 & Round 8.
- Stuff the head.
- Use the long end for the drawstring close and for needle sculpting to tuck the eyes, if desired.
- Set the head aside until Round 4 of the body (if jointing the neck) or until the body is completed (if sewing the head in place).

HANDS and FEET (Make 4)

- Working in continuous rounds
- Working with Green yarn (Tea Leaf)

Round 1: sc 6 in a magic ring (6)
Round 2: (sc inc in ea st) around (12)
Round 3: (sc in BLO of ea st) around (12)
Round 4 - Round 5: (sc in ea st) around (12)
Round 6: (sc2tog) six times (6)

- Tuck the end into the foot
- Lightly stuff.
- Pull up three loops evenly spaced across the top opening of the foot; this closes the foot and provides the 3 starting loops for your I-cord.
- Do not FO.
- Use the three loops to start the arms/legs.

I-CORD ARMS and LEGS (Make 4)

- Working in rows
- Do NOT turn

Row 1: Drop 2 loops (pinching them so they don't unravel), ch 1, pick up 2nd loop & ch 1, pick up last loop & ch 1
Row 2 - Row 7: repeat Row 1

- To finish, yo, pull through all three, yo, pull through one.
- Add the claws.

CLAWS

- Pointing hook towards the leg
- Root in center 4 front loops
- Working with Aran yarn

Round 1: join with a sl st, *ch 3, sl st in back bump of 3rd ch from the hook, sl st in next available front loop of foot,* repeat from * to * two more times

- FO and hide the ends inside the foot.
- Set aside until Round 3 & Round 15 of the body.

TAIL

- Working from tip to base
- Working in continuous rounds
- Working with Green yarn (Tea Leaf)

Round 1: sc 4 in a magic ring (4)
Round 2 - Round 3: (sc in ea st) around (4)
Round 4: (sc in next st, sc inc) around (6)

- FO.
- Do not stuff.
- Set aside until Round 15 of the body.

BODY

- Working from the neck down
- Working in continuous rounds
- Working with Green yarn (Tea Leaf)

Round 1: sc 6 in a magic ring (6)
Round 2: (sc inc) around (12)
Round 3: sc 3, sc 2 while joining 1st arm, sc 4, sc 2 while joining 2nd arm, sc 1 (12)
Round 4: (sc in ea st) around (12)
- Install cotter pin if jointing the neck
Round 5: (sc in ea st) around (12)
Round 6: (sc in the next 3 sts, sc inc) around (15)
Round 7: (sc in ea st) around (15)
Round 8: (sc in the next 4 sts, sc inc) around (18)
Round 9: (sc in the next 5 sts, sc inc) around (21)
Round 10 - Round 11: (sc in ea st) around (21)
Round 12: (sc in the next 6 sts, sc inc) around (24)
Round 13: (sc in the next 7 sts, sc inc) around (27)
Round 14: (sc in ea st) around (27)
Round 15: sc 3, sc 3 while joining tail, sc 8, sc 2 while joining 1st leg, sc 5, sc 2 while joining 2nd leg, sc 4 (27)
Round 16: (sc in the next st, sc2tog) around (18)
- Stuff the body
Round 17: repeat round 16 (12)
Round 18: (sc2tog) around (6)

- FO & drawstring close.
- Sew the head to the body if you didn't joint the neck.

INNER SHELL

- Working in continuous rounds
- Working with Yellow yarn (Lemon)

Round 1: sc 6 into a magic ring (6)
Round 2: (sc inc) around (12)
Round 3: (sc in next 1 sts, sc inc) around (18)
Round 4: (sc in next 2 sts, sc inc) around (24)
Round 5: (sc in next 3 sts, sc inc) around (30)
Round 6: (sc in next 4 sts, sc inc) around (36)
Round 7: (sc in next 5 sts, sc inc) around (42)

- Sl st in 1st st of round.
- FO.
- Set aside until the outer shell is completed.

OUTER SHELL

- Starting with Green yarn (Tea Leaf)
- Sl st, ch 1, between rounds
- To cc sl st in 1st st of round, FO and join new color with a sc in any st

Round 1: sc 6 into a magic ring (6)
Round 2: (sc inc) around (12)
- Cc to Yellow (lemon)
Round 3: (sc in next st, sc inc) around (18)
- Cc to Green (tea Leaf)
Round 4: (sc in next 2 sts, sc inc) around (24)
Round 5: (sc in next 3 sts, sc inc) around (30)
- Cc to Yellow (Lemon)
Round 6: (sc in next 5 sts, fpdc to yellow round) around - Do Not skip the st behind the fpdc (36)
- Cc to Green (tea Leaf)
Round 7: (sc in next 5 sts, sc inc) around (42)
Round 8: (sc) around (42)

- Sl st in 1st st of round.
- FO.
- Continue on to the next section to join the shells.

For Fpdc- YO, reach down inserting hook under post

Yarn over

Pull up a loop

Complete as you would a regular double crochet stitch

JOINING SHELLS

- With wrong side of shells facing each other and right sides showing
- Joining with a single crochet through both panels
- Joining directly above any fpdc on the outer shell.
- Hiding ends inside as you go.
- Do NOT stuff.
- Working with Yellow yarn (Lemon)
- Working in continuous rounds

Round 1: sc 4, fpdc to yellow round, sc 7, fpdc, sc 14, fpdc, sc 7, fpdc, sc 10 (46)
Round 2: FLO sc 16, hdc in next 3 sts, dc 3 in next st, hdc in next 3 sts, FLO sc 23 (48)

- FO.
- Do an invisible join.

Joining the edges, starting
directly above any fpdc

TUMMY PLATE

- Joining in the 12th available back loop on the inside of the shell
- Working up towards the top of the shell
- Ch 1 to turn (unless otherwise indicated). This does NOT count as a stitch
- Working in Yellow (Lemon)

Row 1: work 7 sl sts while joining to the shell
- Place all sts in BLO for the rest of the rows

Row 2: (sl st) across (7)

Row 3: sl st inc, sl st in next 5 sts, sl st inc (9)

Row 4 - Row 5: (sl st) across (9)

Row 6: sl st inc, sl st in next 7 sts, sl st inc (11)

Row 7 - Row 9: (sl st) across (11)

Row 10: sl st in next 10 sts, sl st inc (12)

Short Row 11: sl st in next 5 sts, leave remaining sts unworked, turn but do NOT ch 1 (5)

Short Row 12: sl st in next 5 sts (5)

Row 13: (sl st) across (12)

Row 14: sl st in next 10 sts, slst2tog (11)

Row 15 - Row 16: (sl st) across (11)

Row 17: slst2tog, sl st in next 7 sts, slst2tog (9)

Row 18 - Row 19: (sl st) across (9)

Row 20: slst2tog, sl st in next 5 sts, slst2tog (7)

Row 21: (sl st) across (7)

Row 22: sl st while joining, starting in 6th available back loop down from the top of the shell

- FO.
- Hide the ends inside the shell.

Start tummy plate by joining sl sts on the inner shell

Complete with st sts down the other side of the shell

Red Heart, Super Saver in Buff with Charcoal tummy plate

To slst2tog in the BLO Insert hook in 1st BLO

Insert hook in next BLO

Yarn over

Pull through all loops on the hook

MATERIALS:

- Worsted weight yarn (medium 4)
  - Red Heart Super Saver in Coral (27.5 g)
  - Red Heart Super Saver in Soft White (8 g)
  - Red Heart Super Saver in Charcoal (6.5 g)
- 4 mm hook
- Stitch marker(s)
- Scissors
- Fiberfill
- 12 mm safety eyes in brown
- Doll-making needle
- Optional: one 3/32" x 1 ½" cotter pin, one 3/32" x 3/16" hitch pin clip, two 3/16" fender washers, two No. 6 countersunk finishing washers, and pliers for bending the cotter pin (if you are doing the jointed neck)

ABBREVIATIONS USED IN THIS FLOPPY:

BLO - Back Loop Only
Cc - Color Change
Ch - Chain
Dc - Double Crochet
Dc2tog - Double Crochet Two Together
Dlst - Double Loop Stitch

Ea - Each
FLO - Front Loop Only
FO - Finish Off
Hdc - Half Double Crochet
Inc - Increase
PM - Place Marker

Sc - Single Crochet
Sc2tog - Single Crochet Two Together
Sl st - Slip Stitch
St(s) - Stitch or Stitches
Tr - Treble
Yo - Yarn Over

Floppy Fox Teaches:

- Double Loop Stitch – pg. 160
- Double Crochet Two Together – pg. 152
- Brushing – pg. 158

EARS (Make 2)

- Working top to bottom
- Working in continuous rounds
- Starting with Dark Grey yarn (Charcoal)

Round 1: 5 sc in a magic ring (5)
Round 2: (sc in ea st) around (5)
Round 3: (sc inc in ea st) around (10)
Round 4: (sc in ea st) around (10)
- Cc to main color (Coral)

Round 5: (sc in the next st, sc inc) around (15)
Round 6: (sc in ea st) around (15)
Round 7: (sc in the next 2 sts, sc inc) around (20)
Round 8: (sc2tog, sc in the next 2 sts) around (15)
Round 9: (sc2tog, sc in 13) around (14)

- FO.
- Do not stuff.
- Set aside until Round 12 of the head.

NOSE

- With Dark Grey yarn (Charcoal)
- Starting and finishing with long tail to use when sewing in place

Row 1: sc 3 into magic ring, pull to close but do not join

- FO.
- Set aside until the head is complete.
- Sew in place with the bottom point of the nose at the center of the magic ring that was used to start the head.

HEAD

- Working from the nose to the back of the head
- Working in continuous rounds
- Starting with White yarn

Round 1: sc 4 in a magic ring (4)
Round 2: (sc inc in each st) around (8)
Round 3 - Round 4: (sc in ea st) around (8)
Round 5: (sc in the next st, sc inc) around (12)
Round 6: (sc in ea st) around (12)
Round 7: (sc in the next 2 sts, sc inc) around (16)
Round 8: cc to Coral (sc 3, sc inc) twice, cc to White, (sc 3, sc inc) twice (20)
Round 9: cc to Coral, sc 4, (sc inc in BLO) twice, sc 4, cc to White, sc inc, sc 8, sc inc (24)
Round 10: cc to Coral, sc in the next 3 sts, (1 hdc, hdc inc) three times, 1 hdc, sc in the next 3 sts, cc to White, sc 4, (sc2tog) two times, sc in remaining 3 sts (25)
- FO with White yarn
- PM in base of 1st and last hdc sts of Round 10

Round 11: (sc in ea st) around (25)
Round 12: sc 7 while joining ear, sc 3, sc 7 while joining ear, sc 8 (25)
Round 13: (sc in ea st) around (25)
Round 14: (sc in the next 3 sts, sc2tog) around (20)
Round 15: (sc in the next 2 sts, sc2tog) around (15)
Round 16: (sc in the next st, sc2tog) around (10)

- FO with a long tail.
- Place eyes at the base of the 1st and last hdc sts (where you placed your stitch markers).
- Place cotter pin (if jointing the neck) at bottom/center between Round 10 & Round 11.
- Stuff the head.
- Use the long end for the drawstring close and for needle sculpting to tuck the eyes, if desired.
- Sew on the nose.
- Move on to Bridge of Nose.

BRIDGE OF NOSE

- With main color yarn (Coral)
- Starting and finishing with long tail to use when sewing in place
- Working in rows
- Join to 1st available front loop from Round 9 of the head, with hook pointing towards the nose

Row 1: sc in ea FLO (2)
Row 2: ch 2, turn, dc2tog (1)

- FO.
- Sew to the face.
- Set the head aside until Round 4 of the body (if jointing the neck) or until the body is completed (if sewing the head in place).

Join in the available front loops between the eyes

Sew the completed flap down to the face

HANDS and ARMS (Make 2)

- Working in continuous rounds
- Starting with the hand and working into the arm
- Working with Dark Grey yarn (Charcoal)

Round 1: 6 sc in a magic ring (6)
Round 2 - Round 3: (sc in ea st) around (6)

- Cc to main color (Coral) in last stitch.
- Tie off and tuck the ends into the hand.
- Do not stuff.
- Pull up two more loops evenly spaced across the opening of the hand; this closes the hand and provides the loops needed to start the I-cord (3 loops on hook).

I-CORD ARMS

- Working in rows
- Do NOT turn

Row 1: Drop 2 loops (pinching them so they don't unravel), ch 1, pick up 2nd loop & ch 1, pick up last loop & ch 1
Row 2 - Row 12: repeat Row 1

- To finish, yo, pull through all three, cut yarn, yo, pull through one.
- Set aside until Round 3 of the body.

FEET and LEGS (Make 2)

- Working in continuous rounds
- Starting with the foot and working into the leg
- Working with Dark Grey yarn (Charcoal)

Round 1: 6 sc in a magic ring (6)
Round 2: (sc inc in ea st) around (12)
Round 3: (sc in ea st) around (12)
Round 4: (sc2tog) six times (6)

- Cc to main color (Coral) in last stitch.
- Tie off and tuck the ends into the foot.
- Do not stuff.
- Pull up two more loops evenly spaced across the opening of the foot; this closes the foot and provides the loops needed to start the I-cord (3 loops on hook).

I-CORD LEGS

- Working in rows
- Do NOT turn

Row 1: Drop 2 loops (pinching them so they don't unravel), ch 1, pick up 2nd loop & ch 1, pick up last loop & ch 1
Row 2 - Row 17: repeat Row 1

- To finish, yo, pull through all three, cut yarn, yo, pull through one.
- Set aside until Round 15 of the body.

129

BIB

- Working in rows
- Working with White yarn (Soft White)
- Starting and finishing with long to tail to use to sew bib to chest

Row 1: ch 5, turn
Row 2: starting in second ch from the hook, (sc in back bumps of ch) across (4)
Row 3: ch 1, turn, **in 1st st**- sc, hdc, dc, **in second st**- tr twice, ch 2, sl st in the 2nd ch from the hook, **in third st**- tr twice, and **in last st**- dc, hdc, sc

- FO.
- Set aside until Round 3 of the body.

TAIL

- Working in continuous round from tip of tail to base
- Starting with White yarn

Round 1: sc 4 in a magic ring (4)
Round 2 - Round 3: (dlst in ea sc) around (4)
Round 4: (2 dlst in ea st) around (8)
Round 5: (dlst in ea st) around (8)
- Sl st in next st, FO
- Cc to main color (Coral)
- join with a sl st in any st
Round 6: (dlst in ea st) around (8)
Round 7: (dlst in the next st, dlst 2 in the next) around (12)
Round 8 - Round 10: (dlst in ea st) around (12)
Round 11: (sk 1, dlst in the next st) around (6)
Round 12 - Round 14: (dlst in ea st) around (6)

- Sl st in next stitch.
- FO.
- Cut all loops, and brush out with a detangling brush.
- Use your scissors to shape as desired.
- Set aside until Round 15 of the body.

BODY

- Working from the neck down
- Working in continuous rounds
- Starting with main color yarn (Coral)

Round 1: sc 6 in a magic ring (6)
Round 2: (sc inc) twice, cc to White, (sc inc) twice, cc to main color (Coral), (sc inc) twice (12)
Round 3: sc 2, sc 2 while joining 1st arm, cc to white, sc 4 while joining the bib, cc to main color (Coral), sc 2 while joining 2nd arm, sc 2 (12)
- FO White yarn and tie to secure
Round 4: (sc in ea st) around (12)
- Install cotter pin if jointing the neck
Round 5: (sc in ea st) around (12)
Round 6: (sc in the next 3 sts, sc inc) around (15)
Round 7: (sc in ea st) around (15)
Round 8: (sc in the next 4 sts, sc inc) around (18)
Round 9: (sc in the next 5 sts, sc inc) around (21)
Round 10 - Round 11: (sc in ea st) around (21)
Round 12: (sc in the next 6 sts, sc inc) around (24)
Round 13: (sc in the next 7 sts, sc inc) around (27)
Round 14: (sc in ea st) around (27)
Round 15: sc 2, sc 3 while joining tail, sc 8, sc 2 while joining 1st leg, sc 5, sc 2 while joining 2nd leg, sc 5 (27)
Round 16: (sc in the next st, sc2tog) around (18)
- Stuff the body
Round 17: repeat round 16 (12)
Round 18: (sc2tog) around (6)

- FO & drawstring close.
- Sew the head to the body if you didn't joint the neck.
- Use long ends from bib to tack the bib down to the chest. Hide the ends in the body.

Floppy Lion

MATERIALS:

- Worsted weight yarn (medium 4)
    - Red Heart Super Saver in Buff (40.5 g)
    - Red Heart Super Saver in Gold (15 g)
    - Red Heart Super Saver in Black for nose (about a 30" length)
- 4 mm hook
- Stitch marker(s)
- Scissors
- Fiberfill
- 12 mm safety eyes in yellow
- Doll-making needle
- Optional: one 3/32" x 1 ½" cotter pin, one 3/32" x 3/16" hitch pin clip, two 3/16" fender washers, two No. 6 countersunk finishing washers, and pliers for bending the cotter pin (if you are doing the jointed neck)

ABBREVIATIONS USED IN THIS FLOPPY:

BLO - Back Loop Only	FO - Finish Off	SSc3tog - Single Crochet Three Together
Cc - Color Change	Hdc - Half Double Crochet	Sk - Skip
Ch - Chain	Inc - Increase	Sl st - Slip Stitch
Dlst - Double Loop Stitch	PM - Place Marker	St(s) - Stitch or Stitches
Ea - Each	Sc - Single Crochet	Yo - Yarn Over
FLO - Front Loop Only	Sc2tog - Single Crochet Two Together	

Floppy Lion Teaches:

. Attaching the wig cap - pg. 136

133

WIG CAP

- With mane color (Gold)
- Starting and finishing with long tail to use when sewing in place
- Working in rows
- Ch 1 to turn, does NOT count as a stitch

Row 1: ch 4, turn
Row 2: sk 1st ch, dlst in the next 3 ch sts, ch 1, turn (3 sets of loops)
Row 3: (sc in ea st) across, ch 1, turn (3)
Row 4: (dlst in ea sc) across, sc in the same st as the last dlst, ch 1, turn (3 sets of loops)
Row 5: sc in the next 3 sts, sc inc in the last st, ch 1, turn (5)
Row 6: (dlst in ea sc) across, sc in the same st as the last dlst, ch 1, turn (5 sets of loops)
Row 7: sc in the next 5 sts, sc inc in the last st, ch 1, turn (7)
Row 8: (dlst in ea sc) across, sc in the same st as the last dlst, ch 1, turn (7 sets of loops)
Row 9: sc in the next 7 sts, sc inc in the last st, ch 1, turn (9)
Row 10: (dlst in ea sc) across, sc in the same st as the last dlst, ch 1, turn (9 sets of loops)
Row 11: sc in the next 9 sts, sc inc in the last st, ch 1, turn (11)
Row 12: (dlst in ea sc) across, ch 1, turn (11 sets of loops)
Row 13: (sc in ea st) across, ch 1, turn (11)
Row 14: (dlst in ea sc) across (11 sets of loops)

- FO, leave a long tail for sewing to the head.
- Set aside until the head is completed.

EARS (Make 2)

- Working from top to base
- Working in continuous rounds
- Working with Buff yarn

Round 1: sc 6 in a magic ring (6)
Round 2: (sc inc in ea st) around (12)
Round 3 - Round 4: (sc into ea st) around (12)

- FO.
- Do not stuff.
- Set aside until Round 10 of the head.

NOSE

- Working with Black yarn
- Starting and finishing with long tail to use when sewing in place

Row 1: sc 3 into magic ring, pull to close but do not join

- FO.
- Set aside until the head is complete.
- Sew in place with the bottom point of the nose at the center of the magic ring that was used to start the head.

HEAD

- Working from the nose to the back of the head
- Working in continuous rounds
- Working with Buff yarn

Round 1: sc 6 in a magic ring (6)
Round 2: (sc inc in ea st) around (12)
Round 3 - Round 4: (sc in ea st) around (12)
Round 5: (in FLO sc in the next 2 sts, FLO sc inc) around (16)
Round 6: (sc in the next 3 sts, sc inc) around (20)
Round 7: (sc in the next 4 sts, sc inc) around (24)
Round 8: sc in the next 3 sts, (1 hdc, hdc inc) three times, 1 hdc, sc in the next 7 sts, (sc2tog) two times, sc in remaining 3 sts (25)
- PM in 1st and last hdc sts and mark the center of the hdc sts of Round 8
Round 9: (sc in ea st) around (25)
Round 10: sc 1, sc 6 while joining ear, sc 3, sc 6 while joining ear, sc 9 (25)
Round 11: (sc in ea st) around (25)
Round 12: (sc in the next 3 sts, sc2tog) around (20)
Round 13: (sc in the next 2 sts, sc2tog) around (15)
Round 14: (sc in the next st, sc2tog) around (10)

- FO with a long tail.
- Place eyes at the base of the 1st and last hdc sts (where you placed your stitch markers).
- Place cotter pin (if jointing the neck) at bottom/center between Round 8 & Round 9.
- Stuff the head.
- Use the long end for the drawstring close and for needle sculpting to tuck the eyes, if desired.
- Sew on the nose.
- Sew on the wig cap with first 3 sts of the wig cap at the top of the hdc sts of the forehead.
- Set the head aside until Round 4 of the body (if jointing the neck) or until the body is completed (if sewing the head in place).

Sew front of cap at the top of the hdc forehead stitches

Wig cap should curve behind the ears...

and across the bottom of the head

TOES (Make 3 per foot: Make 2 and FO, Make 1 and do NOT FO)

- Working in continuous rounds
- Working with Buff yarn

Round 1: 4 sc in a magic ring (4)
Round 2: (sc inc in ea st) around (8)
Round 3: (sc in ea st) around (8)
Round 4: (sc2tog) around (4)

- Tuck the end into toe.
- Do not stuff.
- FO on first two toes.
- Do NOT FO on third toe; continue onto the foot.

PUTTING TOES TOGETHER AND FORMING THE FOOT (Make 4)

- With the last toe still on the hook (this will now be referred to as the first toe) and using its working yarn

Round 5: sc in two sc sts of middle toe, sc in 4 sc sts of last toe, moving back along the other side of the toes, sc in 2 sc sts of the middle toe, sc in the 4 sc sts of the first toe (12)
Round 6: (sc inc in ea st) aorund (24)
Round 7: (sc in ea st) around (24)
Round 8: (sc2tog) around (12)
Round 9: (sc2tog) around (6)

- Do NOT FO.
- Lightly stuff the foot.
- Pull up two more loops evenly spaced across the opening of the foot; this closes the foot and provides the loops needed to start the I-cord (3 loops on the hook).
- Move on to the arm or leg.

I-CORD ARMS (Make 2)

- Working in rows
- Do NOT turn

Row 1: Drop 2 loops (pinching them so they don't unravel), ch 1, pick up 2nd loop & ch 1, pick up last loop & ch 1
Row 2 - Row 10: repeat Row 1

- To finish, yo, pull through all three, cut yarn, yo, pull through one.
- Set aside until Round 3 of the body.

I-CORD LEGS (Make 2)

- Working in rows
- Do NOT turn

Row 1: Drop 2 loops (pinching them so they don't unravel), ch 1, pick up 2nd loop & ch 1, pick up last loop & ch 1
Row 2 - Row 15: repeat Row 1

- To finish, yo, pull through all three, cut yarn, yo, pull through one.
- Set aside until Round 15 of the body.

BODY

- Working in continuous rounds
- Working inside out to begin with, so that your loops are on the outside of the body (Don't sweat this, just start as normal and let it happen.)
- Starting in mane color (Gold) forming the neck and bib

Round 1: sc 6 in a magic ring (6)
Round 2: (sc inc) around (12)
Round 3: dlst 3, sc 2 while joining 1st arm, dlst 4, sc 2 while joining 2nd arm, dlst 1 (12)
Round 4: (dlst in ea st) around (12)
- Install cotter pin if jointing the neck
Round 5: (dlst in the next 3 sts, dlst inc) around (15)
Round 6: (sc in ea st) around (15)
Round 7: (dlst in BLO of the next 5 sts), leave the remaining 10 sts unworked, ch 1 turn (5)
Round 8: sc2tog, sc in next st, sc2tog, ch 1, turn (3)
Round 9: (dlst in ea st) across, ch 1, turn (3)
Round 10: sc3tog, ch 1, turn (1)
Round 11: dlst in the one remaining st (1)
- FO with a long tail to use to tack down the bib once the body is finished
- Cc to body color (Buff)
- Working as you normally would with the right side of your work facing out
- Work the 1st round of the body color behind the bib, in the available loops
Round 12: joining in the first available BLO from round 6, BLO sc in the 5 sts behind the bib, sc in the next 10 sts of round 6 (15)
Round 13: (sc in the next 4 sts, sc inc) around (18)
Round 14: (sc in the next 5 sts, sc inc) around (21)
Round 15 - Round 16: (sc in ea st) around (21)
Round 17: (sc in the next 6 sts, sc inc) around (24)
Round 18: (sc in the next 7 sts, sc inc) around (27)
Round 19 - Round 21: (sc in ea st) around (27)
Round 22: sc 2 while joining 1st leg, sc 5, sc 2 while joining 2nd leg, sc 18 (27)
Round 23: (sc in the next st, sc2tog) around (18)
- Stuff the body
Round 24: repeat round 16 (12)
Round 25: (sc2tog) around (6)

- FO & drawstring close.
- Sew the head to the body if you didn't joint the neck.
- Sew the bib down to the chest.
- Cut all the loops and brush his mane. (Be careful not to snag his legs.)

Join new color in 1st available loop behind the bib

Then continue around the unworked sts of round 6

TAIL

- Working with Buff colored yarn
- Start with 2 strands of yarn, about a two-foot length.
- Fold in half.
- Insert the hook through the stitch in the center of the bum at Round 16.
- Pull yarn through at the half-way fold point in the yarn.
- Put them together and run them as one length doubled (4 strands).

Row 1: with all 4 strands of yarn ch 6

- Yo, pull through all the way.
- Push your crochet hook through the last chain stitch of the tail.
- Now using gold-colored yarn
- Pull through 4 more 6" stands, folded in half, this creates a loop, pull all ends through the loop and pull tight.
- Cut to desired length, brush and shape.

For the end of the tail, pull through four more stands

Pull all ends through the loop to create the tail fringe

Pattern excerpt taken from Floppy Chihuahua.

EARS (Make 2)

It will be indicated here if you need to make more than one.

- Working top to bottom
- Working in continuous rounds

These points will aid you in the making of each part.

Round 1: 5 sc in magic ring (5)
Round 2: (sc in ea st) around (5)
Round 3: (sc inc in ea st) around (10)
Round 4: (sc in ea st) around (10)
Round 5: (sc in the next st, sc inc) around (15)
Round 6: (sc in ea st) around (15)
Round 7: (sc in the next 2 sts, sc inc) around (20)
Round 8: (sc2tog, sc in the next 2 sts) around (15)
Round 9: sc2tog, sc 13 (14)

Keep track of the Round or Row numbers.

Use the abbreviation key to follow the patterns. Parentheses indicate a sequence of repetition: "(sc in the next st, sc inc)" means, "single crochet in the next stitch, single crochet increase.

This indicates how many times you will repeat the sequence within the round. The word "around" means the sequence repeats for the whole round.

- FO
- Do not stuff.
- Set aside until Round 10 of the head for short-nosed chihuahua.
- Set aside until Round 12 of the head for long-nosed chihuahua.

The numbers in parentheses indicate the total number of stitches you should have when you finish that row or round.

These points will aid you in finishing off each part and tell you what to do next.

Crochet Slang 101

CROJO-

Crochet mojo

I-Cord

The i-cord is what makes the Floppies what they are . . . "The Floppies!" They have a unique and comical look that kids love. Their rope limbs flop around wildly as they swing through the air, propelled by a happy child. They are quick and easy once you get the hang of it.

I-CORD TIPS:

- Do NOT turn your work.
- If you are having trouble holding your loose loops, try using a knitting needle, an additional crochet hook, or a large darning needle to keep the stitches from unraveling while you work.
- If you are unable to master the crocheted I-cord, there are other options. An I-cord knitter, available in craft stores and online, will also do the trick, though you will have to add the feet separately.

Starting an I-cord (Chain 3 Method)

Chain 3

Pull up loop though 2nd chain from the hook

Pull up loop though 3rd chain from the hook

Joining the I-cord

For the majority of the Floppies, the feet and hands are made and then 3 stitches are simply picked up across the top of the hand or foot. These three stitches work to close the hand or foot, and serve as the starting point for the I-cord.

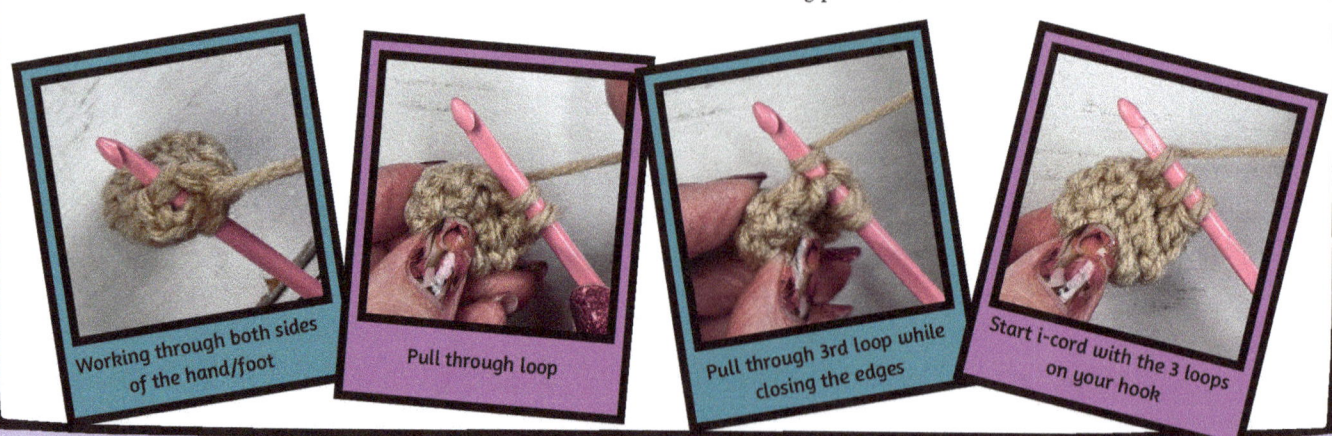

Working through both sides of the hand/foot

Pull through loop

Pull through 3rd loop while closing the edges

Start i-cord with the 3 loops on your hook

Continuing the I-Cord

Whether the I-cord is started by picking up loops through the top of the hand or foot, or by picking up loops through a starting chain, the continuation is the same. You will be working with the three available loops.

Drop 2 stitches, pinch to keep them from unraveling

Chain 1

Pick up the dropped loop closest to the hook

Chain 1

Pick up the last dropped loop

Chain 1

Repeat until desired length

Finishing the I-Cord

Finishing the I-cord is simply a matter of pulling all the loops together and finishing off.

Yarn over and pull through all 3 loops

Yarn over and pull through loop

Pull end through

The First Step - Attaching the Yarn to the Hook

Attach the yarn to your hook with either a magic circle or a simple slip knot. This is the first step before you can do anything. Shown below is how to get the slip knot onto your hook.

Create a loop around your hook

Pull working end of yarn though center of the loop

Pull to tighten the loop onto the hook

Ch = Chain

The chain stitch is commonly used as a foundation when working in rows. It is also used to make the tail for Floppy Mouse, Elephant, and Lion.

With slip stitch on the hook yarn over

Pull through loop to complete a chain stitch

Repeat yarn over and pull through to continue chain

Back Bump

The back bump is located on the chain stitch. It is used to achieve a neater edge.

This is the back bump of the chain

Insert hook through the back bump

Complete the stitch as usual

Both Loops (The 'V')

We almost always work our stitches through the top of both the front and back loop. The front and back loop together form a "V" shape. Unless the pattern calls for using the BLO (back loop only) or the FLO (front loop only), this will be where you work the stitch.

We work most of our stitches under the "V" shape

MR = Magic Ring

The Magic Ring, or Magic Circle, is the most common way to begin a part of an amigurumi that is worked in the round. When done correctly, it secures and cinches the yarn tightly so there is no hole. If you cannot figure out how to create the magic circle, an alternative is to chain two and work the stitches into the first chain. You can use the non-working end of your yarn to sew up any hole that might be present.

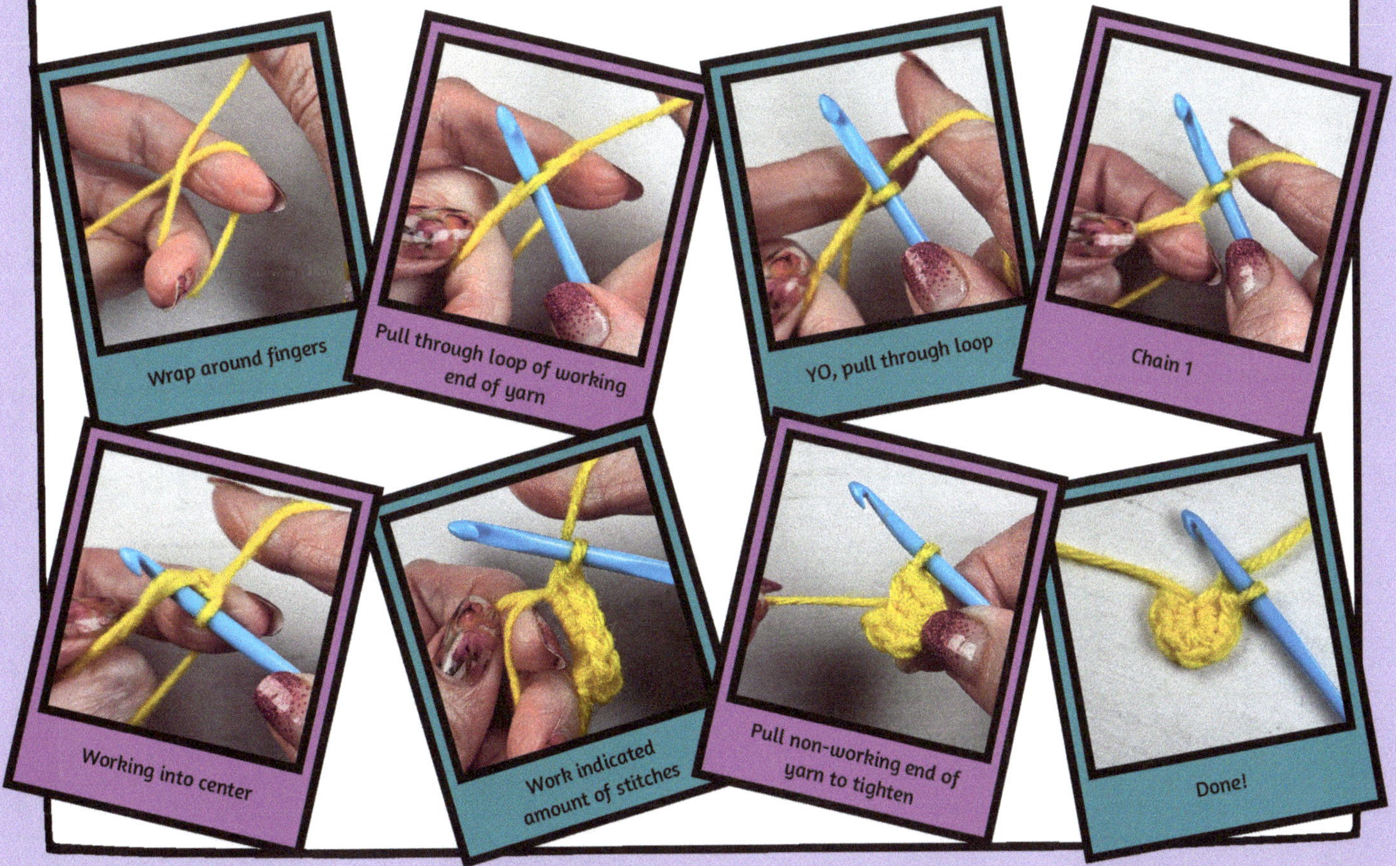

Wrap around fingers

Pull through loop of working end of yarn

YO, pull through loop

Chain 1

Working into center

Work indicated amount of stitches

Pull non-working end of yarn to tighten

Done!

Continuous Rounds

Once the magic ring is completed, it is easy to continue working in a spiral. This is known as working in Continuous Rounds, and it is the method used throughout this book. The example given below is for starting a ring with 6 single crochet stitches. If the starting ring has a different number of stitches, simply count backward from the hook the number of stitches in your magic ring to find your starting point.

Tip: Count backward from your hook to find starting st

Insert hook in 6th stitch from the hook

Yarn over and pull though a loop

Yarn over and pull through both loops on the hook

First sc completed

Place marker in the stitch just created

- You are now ready to work in Rounds.
- The marker is in the first stitch of the Round.

Right Side (RS) and Wrong Side (WS)

Right side and wrong side simply refers to the front and back of the fabric.

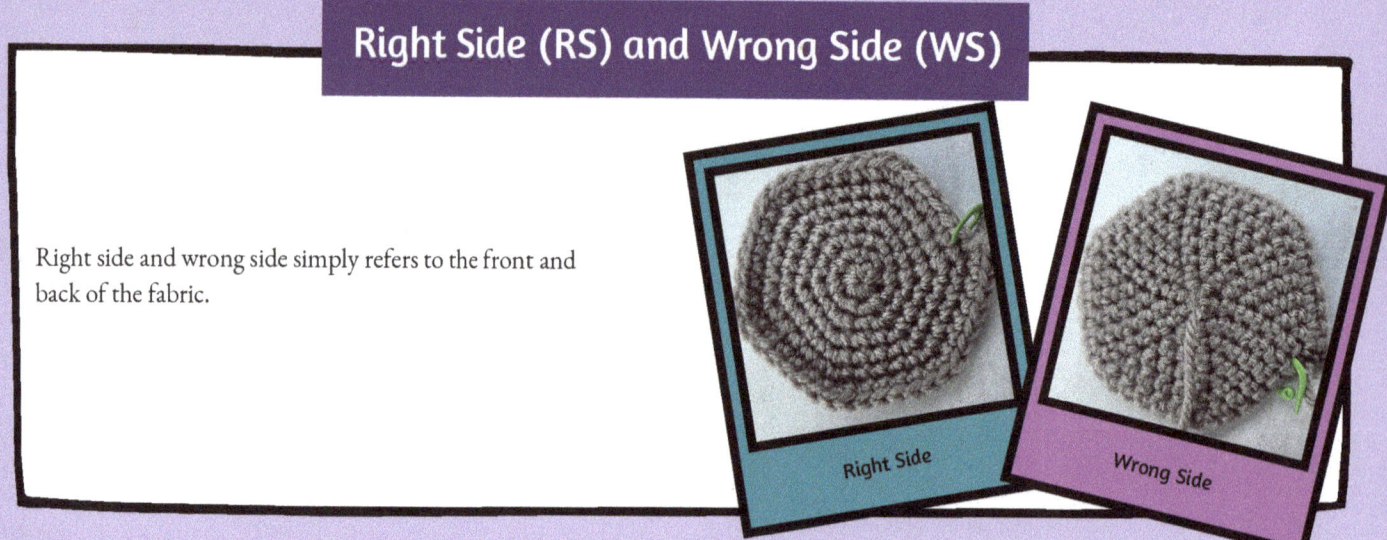

Right Side

Wrong Side

FLO = Front Loop Only

The front loop is the loop closest to you

Working through only the front loop

Complete the stitch as you normally would

BLO = Back Loop Only

The back loop is the loop farther away from you

Working through only the back loop

Complete the stitch as you normally would

The 3rd Loop

The 3rd loop is the horizontal bar behind the top of a hdc st

Working through only the 3rd loop

Complete the stitch, this pushes the top of the hdc st forward

SC = Single Crochet

The Single Crochet stitch is the main stitch used in all amigurumi.

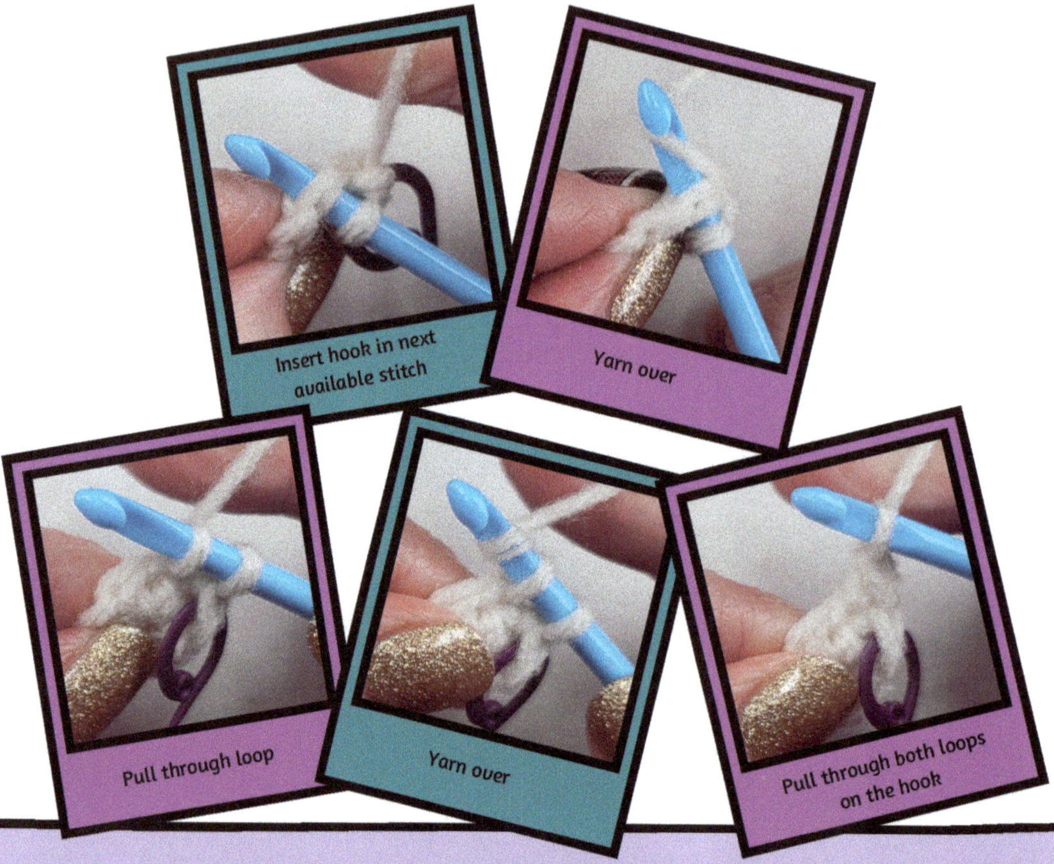

Insert hook in next available stitch

Yarn over

Pull through loop

Yarn over

Pull through both loops on the hook

SC INC = Single Crochet Increase

A Single Crochet Increase is worked by placing two single crochet stitches into the same stitch.

Work 2 sc into the same stitch to increase

SC2TOG = Single Crochet 2 Together (Invisible)

Single Crochet 2 Together (or Single Crochet Decrease) is used to decrease the number of stitches in a round or a row. Invisible decrease is shown in this tutorial. It is advisable to use Invisible Decrease in amigurumi as it creates a smaller hole in the fabric.

Pick up the front loop of the stitch

Pick up the front loop of the next stitch

Yarn over

Pull through loop

Yarn over

Complete single crochet stitch

SC3TOG = Single Crochet 3 Together

Single Crochet 3 Together is exactly what it sounds like. You will follow the steps for sc2tog except you will work it over three stitches instead of two.

Working through 3 stitches

Yo, Pull through 3, Yo, Pull through 2

SC2TOG = Single Crochet 2 Together (Regular)

There are times when a regular Single Crochet 2 Together is preferable, such as in Floppy Pig's ear, where we use it over the ends of the rows to create a bend in the ear (shown below).

Insert hook

Pull up a loop

Insert hook in next stitch

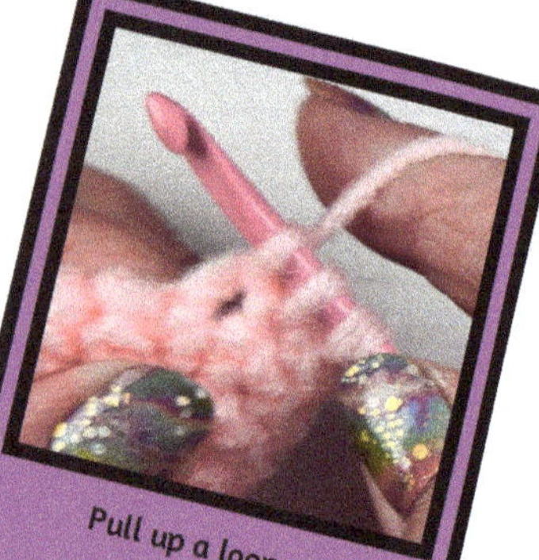

Pull up a loop

Yarn over

Pull through all loops on the hook

Drop Stitch

Drop Stitches are achieved by reaching down to a previous round or row. Other than reaching down, or "dropping" to a previous row, the stitch is completed like a usual stitch.

Insert the hook through the previous round/row

Reaching behind on the wrong side... hook your yarn

Pull it though to the right side and up to height

Complete Stitch as usual

150

HDC = Half Double Crochet

Half Double Crochet is used sparingly as a shaping technique in amigurumi. In the Floppies, I use them in increases over the bridge of the nose to add a bit of easy shaping in a fairly small space.

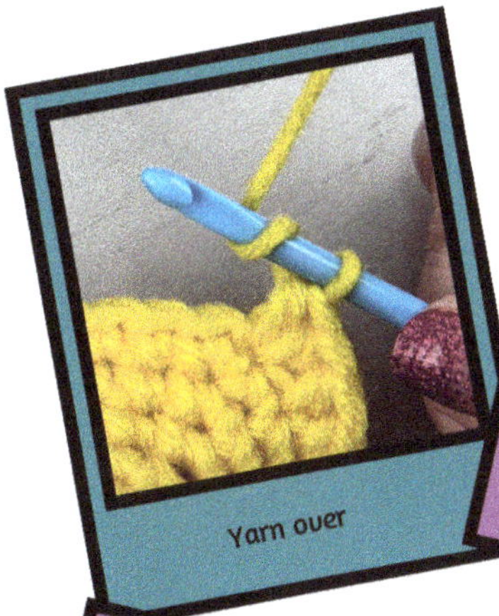

Yarn over

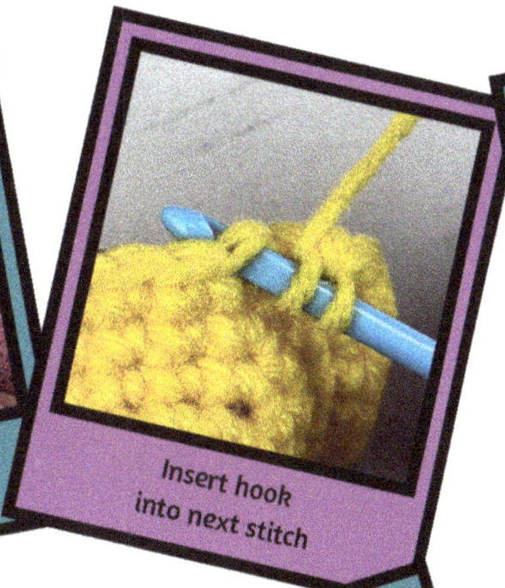

Insert hook into next stitch

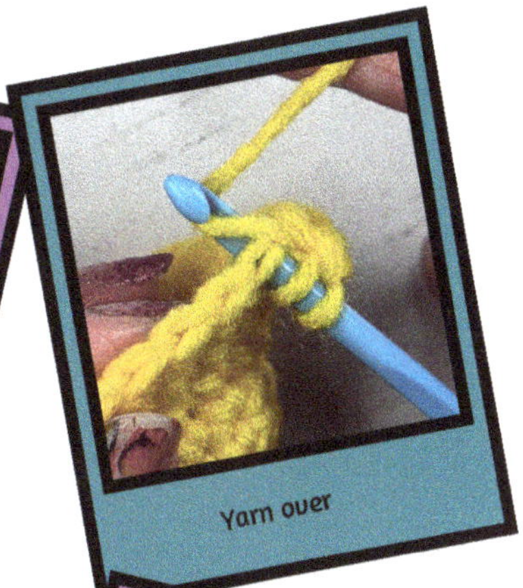

Yarn over

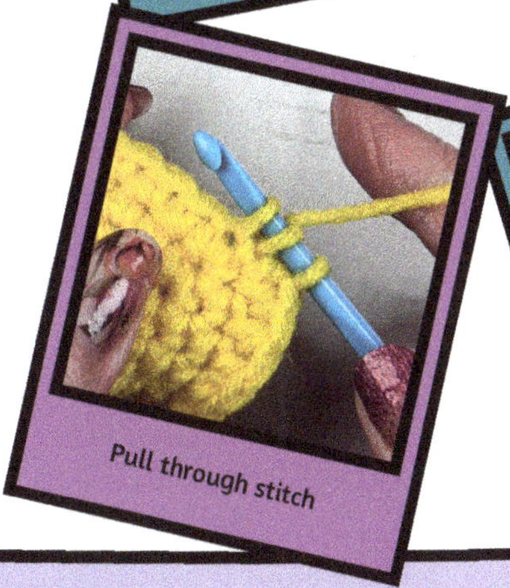

Pull through stitch

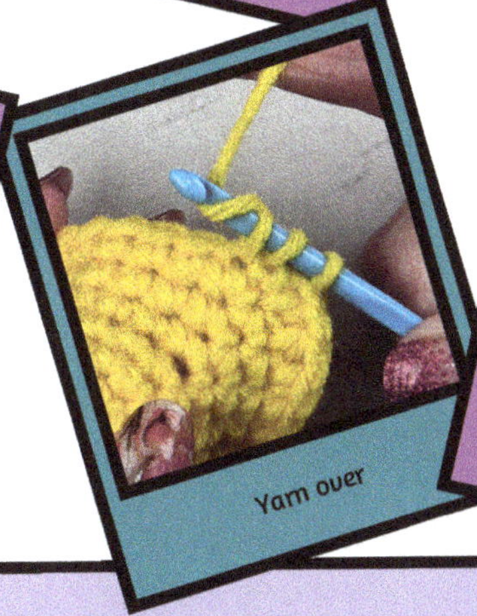

Yarn over

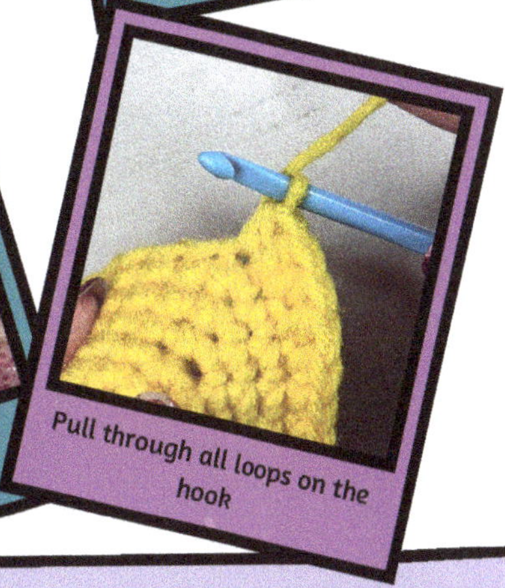

Pull through all loops on the hook

HDC INC = Half Double Crochet Increase

A Half Double Crochet Increase is worked by placing two half double crochet stitches into the same stitch.

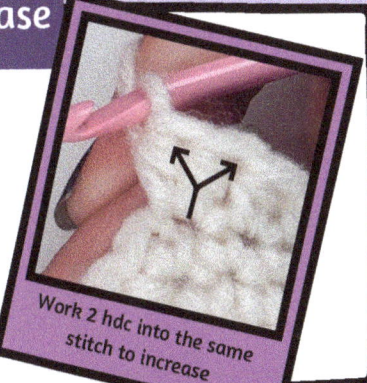

Work 2 hdc into the same stitch to increase

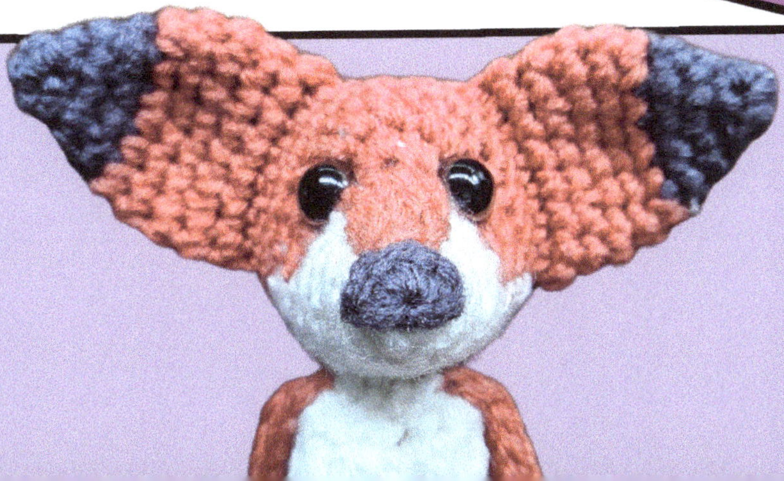

DC = Double Crochet

The Double Crochet stitch is slightly taller than the Half Double Crochet stitch. It is found in the tails and wings of the Floppies and is used to make Floppy Sloth's nose.

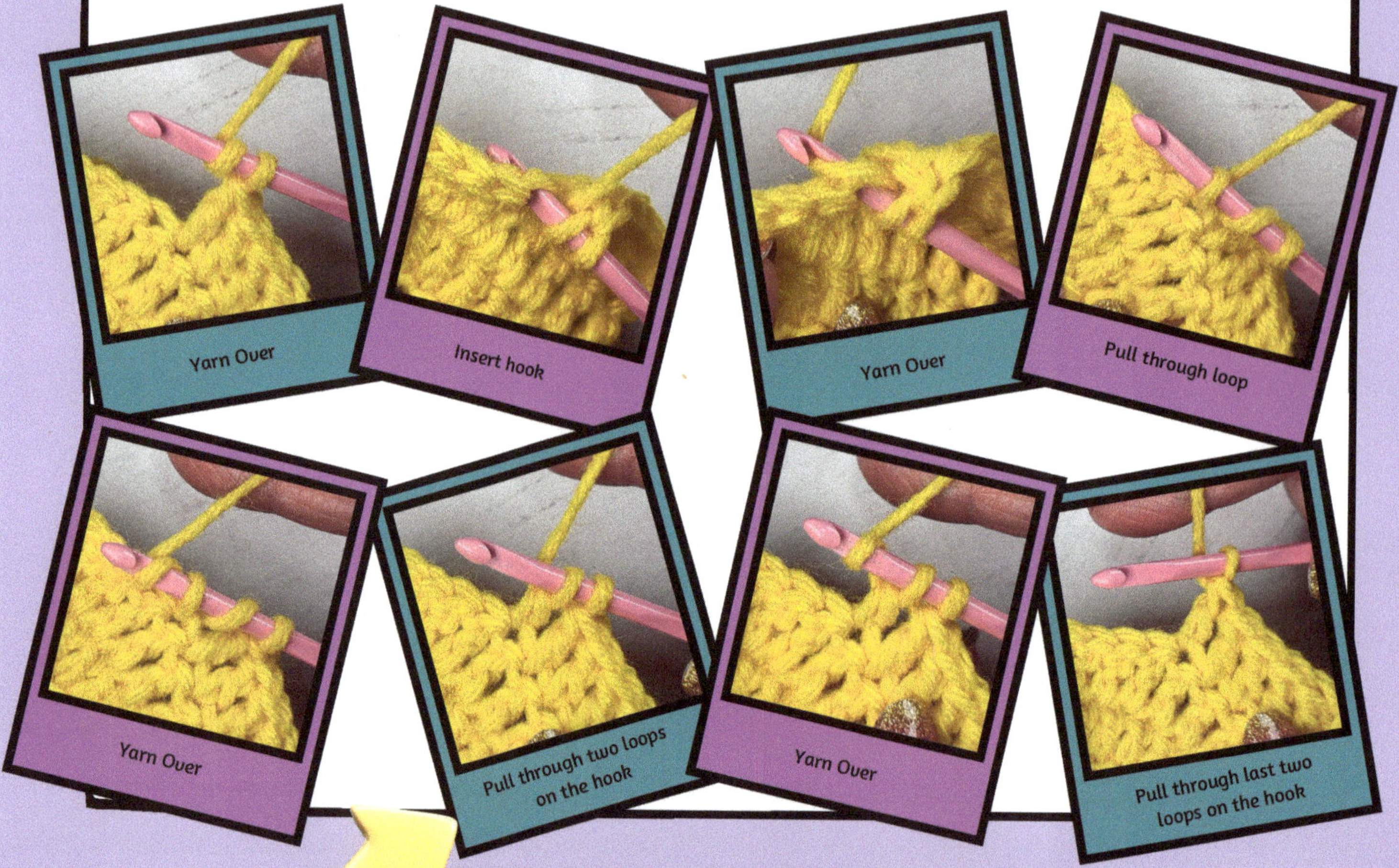

Yarn Over

Insert hook

Yarn Over

Pull through loop

Yarn Over

Pull through two loops on the hook

Yarn Over

Pull through last two loops on the hook

DC2TOG = Double Crochet Two Together

To Double Crochet Two Together, work two double crochet stitches to the step indicated by the arrow, then complete the steps below.

Work two dc stitches without completing either

There will be 3 loops on the hook, yarn over...

and pull through all loops

Tr = Treble Stitch

The Treble Stitch is the next step up in height from the Double Crochet Stitch. It is similar to the Double Crochet, and has an additional wrap around and an additional pull through.

Wrap yarn around the hook twice

Insert hook through stitch

Yarn Over

Pull through loop

Yarn Over

Pull through two loops on the hook

Yarn Over

Pull through two loops on the hook

Yarn Over

Pull through last two loops on the hook

153

Joining with a Single Crochet Stitch

One of the easiest ways to join a new color to a completed part (like Teddy Bear's muzzle) is with a single crochet stitch.

With new color, start with a slip stitch on your hook

Insert the hook in the stitch you wish to join

Yarn over

Pull through loop

Complete the single crochet stitch

Continue to work in rounds as usual

Invisible Join

When you are finishing off a part with single crochet stitches that have been worked in the round, you may want to complete the round with an Invisible Join. This is a bit tidier than a regular slip stitch join to finish off.

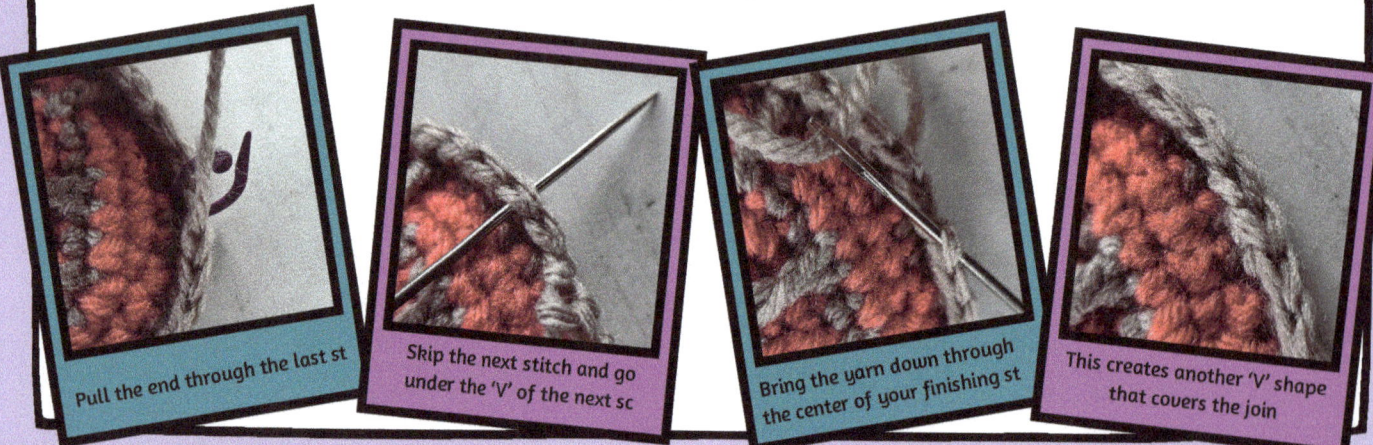

Pull the end through the last st

Skip the next stitch and go under the 'V' of the next sc

Bring the yarn down through the center of your finishing st

This creates another 'V' shape that covers the join

Changing Colors

This method can be used for any stitch (ie: sc, hdc, dc). Simply change the color before completing the last step of the stitch. If you are joining a new color, you can knot the ends together inside the amigurumi to make everything secure. If you are changing back and forth between colors, you can carry or drop the yarn as you go.

Stop one step short of completing the last stitch

Pick up the next color with your hook...

and complete the stitch

If you are joining a new color, knot the ends together inside

Continue to work stitches as you normally would

Carrying the Yarn

With projects that have multiple color changes, it is better to carry the yarn, rather than cut it and start the new color again a few stitches later. If you are working in the round, and only changing color for a few stitches, you can also "drop" the yarn and simply pick it up when you change back. This leaves the loose strands inside the project. If you are working in rows, you will need to carry the yarn.

Carry the yarn by laying it on top of the stitches

Work around the yarn that is being carried

Complete the stitch as usual

Sl st = Slip Stitch

Slip Stitches are used in numerous ways in amigurumi. In the Floppies, they are often used to finish off a part. Adding a slip stitch helps to even out the edge so there is no noticeable step between the old and new color, or at the end of a piece. Slip Stitches are also used in shaping wings and toes.

Insert hook through stitch

Yarn over

Pull through all the loops on the hook

Joining with a Slip Stitch

We join with a Slip Stitch (sl st) when we don't want the height of a single crochet. A slip stitch brings your starting point down to the level of the fabric you are joining. The example shown is from Floppy Tortoise, where we are joining in the unworked front loops to add the toes.

Insert hook through the stitch you wish to join to...

Pull through a loop

Yarn over, and pull through both strands of yarn

Pull the non-working end all the way through

Tighten the loop down on the hook

156

Working in Rows

We typically Work in Rows to create flat parts, such as wings. We work across the piece and then chain up to turn. Very often the turning chain is not counted as part of the overall stitch count; it can be helpful to think of turning your work as turning the page of a book, with the hook being the pivot point or the spine.

Simple rows of single crochet stitches

Chain 1

Turn as you would the page of a book

Insert hook in the top of the next available stitch

Complete your stitch, in this case a single crochet

Short Rows

Short Rows, simply put, is when we stop short of completing a row or round. We leave stitches from that row unworked, and often go back and pick those stitches up a few rows later. In amigurumi this is usually done to create a fold, bend, or curve in the work; however, it can also be used to shorten a row, or transition from rounds to rows while avoiding an unnecessary join in the piece.

Stopping the round short, leaving stitches unworked

Chain up and turn like a regular row

Example shown is Floppy Pig's ear

Crocheting the Ends of a Row

On the end of the wings for Floppy Duck and Butterfly, we crochet up the inside edge of the wing and pull in the pleats of the wing to create a bit more shape. It is done by working through the turning chains at the end of the rows.

The wing before the side sts have been added

Working into the turning chain at the end of the row...

and each turning chain up the edge

Then into the 1st st of the starting chain

This completes the wing and creates a rounded bottom edge

Brushing

Brushing is done on the Fox's tail and Lion's mane to create a fur-type appearance. A plastic detangling brush works well when creating a fur look with the double-loop stitch. Use both a brushing and scrubbing motion.

Cut all the loops of your double loop stitches

Then brush and expect some yarn shedding

Finish brushing and trim to shape with scissors

Puff Stitch (Antennae and Toes)

The antennae for Floppy Alien, Bumble Bee, and Butterfly, as well as the toes for Floppy Frog, are all done in the same manner.

Yarn Over

Insert hook in back bump of 2nd chain from the hook

Yarn Over

Pull through loop

Repeat last 4 steps and yarn over again

Pull through all 5 loops on the hook

Insert hook in same st (2nd ch form hook) and yarn over

Slip stitch to complete the puff

Working Around the Chain

For the antennae in this book, you will be asked to crochet Around the Chain. It is exactly what it sounds like. Work your stitches around, and not through the chain. It will then be secured with the last stitch so the stitches don't slide off the chain.

Working around, not through, the chain

Complete the indicated number of sc stitches

Work the last stitch through the last chain

This completes the antenna

Dlst = Double Loop Stitch

The Double Loop Stitch makes great fur for our amigurumi animals. It is worked inside-out with the loops forming on the wrong side (back) of the fabric.

Insert hook pointing to the outside of the work

Wrap yarn around your finger twice

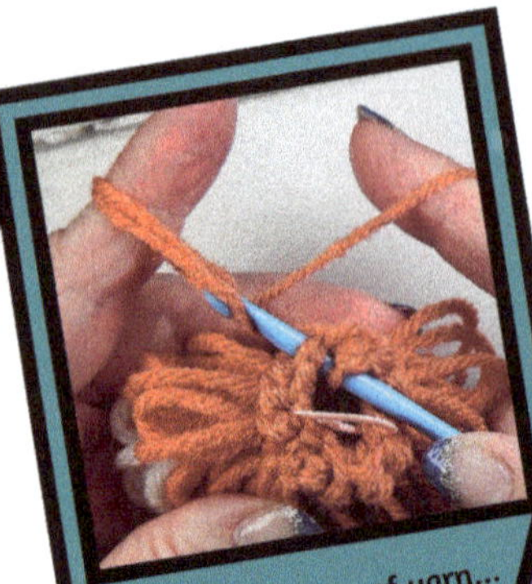

Pick up all loops of yarn...

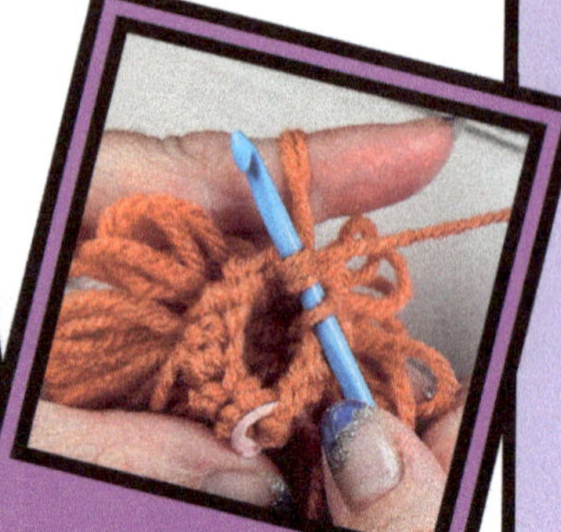

and pull through

Yarn over

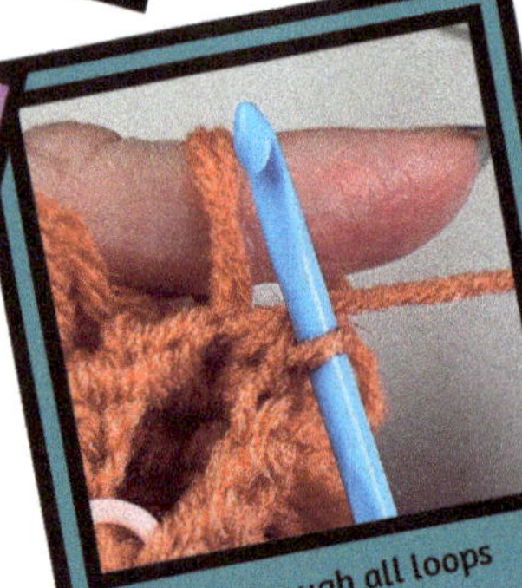

Pull through all loops on the hook

Remove your finger from the loops and repeat for next dlst

Working in Available Front Loops

A few times throughout this book, we will work the back loops only, leaving the Front Loops available to work later. We do this for Floppy Tortoise's Claws, and for the scallops on Floppy Flamingo's wings.

Working along the available front loops

Work the indicated stitches as you normally would

Eye Placement

The eyes for all the Floppies in this book are placed at the base of either the 1st and last hdc, or the 2nd and 2nd-to-last hdc. Eye placement is indicated in the 'Head' section of each pattern. A scrap piece of yarn works well for marking the eye placement.

Place here for 1st and last hdc

Place here for 2nd and 2nd to last hdc

Safety Eyes

Safety Eyes are used in toys for a quick, easy, professional look. However, it is important to note that they can pose a choking risk to young children. Other options include embroidery, crochet, or needle felting the eyes.

Snap together with the concave side facing the back of the eye

Do NOT place with the convex side facing the back of the eye

Stuffing

The most popular Stuffing used in amigurumi is Poly-fil. However, you can also use shredded foam filling or Poly-Pellets. If using Poly-Pellets, you will need to contain them in a stocking, or sew them into tiny pouches. This is known as a "Stuffing Bomb." Otherwise, they will work their way out between your stitches.

Resist the urge to over-stuff. Not only will your stuffing show through the stitches, and cause the shaping to be lost, but it will also stretch the yarn over time and affect the longevity of your piece. Stuffing should be firm but still have give.

Ears

The Ear placement is included in the "Head" section of each pattern. The ears are attached as you are working the round.

Insert the hook through both sides of the ear...

and though the working round of the head

Yarn over

Pull through all three layers

Complete the stitch

Continue until the ear is attached

Repeat the same steps on the other ear

Joining Toes

Toes are joined by working around the available stitches at the top of each toe. Start with the first toe, either still on the hook, or by joining a new color. Then work the indicated amount of stitches on the middle toe(s). Continue around all stitches of the last toe, then back across the stitches on the other side of the middle toe(s). Complete the join by crocheting the available stitches of the first toe. From that point, continue to work in the round to complete the rest of the foot.

With 1st toe on the hook, work stitches of the middle toe(s)

Work all the way around the last toe

Work stitches on opposite side of the middle toe(s)

Complete the round by working the stitches of the 1st toe

Closing Pieces

Most pieces are closed with a "Drawstring close." You may have a personal preference as to how this should be done, and that is fine. Shown here are the two most common methods.

OPTION 1

Weave back and forth under the stiches

Pull closed

Knot and bring the end in against the knot

Hide end inside the piece

OPTION 2

Whip stitch in front loop only

Pull closed and fasten off

As you can see, there is little difference, and they are both equally secure.

Tying Off (The Knot)

Often overlooked in amigurumi tutorials is how to properly Tie Off your pieces. Many people simply hide the ends inside their animal and think that is good enough; however, yarn has an incredible ability to wiggle free over time. Knots are easily hidden if pressed firmly against the fabric and add durability to your finished piece.

Work around a post close to the final stitch

Pull through until you have a small loop

Insert needle, pull loop tight

Place thumb firmly over the needle

Pull the yarn through while holding pressure

Now you have a knot that's tight to the fabric

Crochet Slang 101

W ork

I n

P rogress

165

Needle Sculpting

Needle Sculpting (also known as Soft Sculpting) is used for shaping, utilizing minor tacking to pull the piece into the desired shape or position. With Needle Sculpting, less is often more. I like to place two tacks on each eye of the Floppies, one at the corners of each eye and one at the base. This sinks the eyes into the fabric and creates more depth.

Bring yarn tail through and out at the bottom

Insert the needle one stitch over

Bring the needle out at the corner of the eye

Go in one stitch up and across the bridge of the nose

Down one stitch and back across the bridge of the nose

Pull to indent

In one stitch over and out bottom center

Pull to indent

Needle in one stitch over and...

out at the corner of the other eye

One stitch over and out at the bottom

Pull to indent

Tie off

Hide the end inside the head and finish off

Noses

The Floppy noses are all attached in pretty much the same way. The starting yarn and the finishing yarn are left long, then used to sew the nose to the face. The starting yarn of the nose is inserted through the magic circle of the head, and the finishing yarn is used to secure the outer edge by sewing along the corresponding row of the face.

A nose, with its starting and finishing ends

Pull end through center of magic ring to place nose

With the other end of yarn, sew around the posts

... and under stitches

Weave back and forth until secured

Bring ends out through same stitch, tie together

Pull knot into head, hide ends inside, and cut

Getting cuter!

Sewing Other Parts Together

All parts can be sewn to the surface in the same way as the nose. A whip stitch can also be used, but the stitches will be slightly more visible.

Use the starting tail to tack the piece in place

Work around the outer edge of the piece

Through the spot you would place the hook when crocheting

... and under the posts of the stitches all the way around

The antennae are joined as you go with one single crochet stitch, then knotted in place for added security.

Push the hook through the bottom of the antenna

With antenna on the hook insert hook through next st of head

Work a single crochet stitch in between the ends of the antenna

The ends of the antenna should be on either side of the sc stitch

Knot the ends together inside the head

Crochet Slang 101

U n
F inished
O bject

Jointed Neck (Cotter Pin)

You can either joint the Floppy's necks, or sew them to the body. If you choose to joint the neck, you will need a quick trip to the hardware store. Each neck joint uses one 3/32" x 1 1/2" cotter pin, one 3/32" x 3/16" hitch pin clip, two 3/16" fender washers, and two No. 6 countersunk finishing washers. The hitch pin is optional, but recommended as it will keep the cotter pin from slipping through the washers if too much pressure is applied. You will also need a pair of needle nose or round nose pliers to roll the prongs down on the cotter pin.

Assemble cotter pin, hitch pin, and washer as shown

Slip cotter pin through center/base stitch of head

Stuff and finish the head

Work body to indicated round

Insert cotter pin through center of magic ring

Thread washers onto cotter pin

Use pliers to roll down the cotter pin

Repeat on other side. Roll down until snug

The I-cord limbs are so quick and easy to crochet in place! They are attached as you make the body, and require no sewing. (My son has torture-tested this method, and it has proven to be very secure. He believes Floppies are made to be swung by their limbs in a propellor-type motion.)

With WS facing push hook through top of the limb

Working through next stitch of the body...

Complete the single crochet stitch

Push hook through stitch at the side of the i-cord

Complete the second single crochet stitch

Repeat same method to attach other limbs

Rip-it
Rip-it
Rip-it

Crochet Slang 101

FROG/FROGGING-

"Ribbit" sounds like "Rip it"
So, when we rip out stitches, we are "Frogging" our work.

Joining Tails (As You Crochet)

When the tail ends with a round opening and is joined as you are stitching the body, it is done in the same way as the ears: The open end is pinched together and both edges are worked right into the stitches of the body.

Insert the hook through both sides of the tail...

and though the working round of the body

Yarn over

Pull through all three layers

Complete the stitch

Continue until the tail is attached

Crochet Slang 101

AMI-

Short for Amigurumi, a knit or crochet toy

171

The head can also be sewn to the body by working around the posts of the body between rows 2 and 3, and around the stitches at the base of the head. Check the head positioning a few times as you go. Work around stitches, being careful not to split the yarn. That way, if you need to unpick, it won't damage your work. A crooked head can add so much character, so have an open mind as you sew around, and don't be too quick to unpick if the head isn't perfectly straight. You can also use pins or a long, thin knitting needle to hold pieces in place as you sew.

Start at the back of the head

Pull yarn straight to see which stitch lines up

Work around the posts of the body...

and around the stitches in the head that line up

Continue all the way around

Work back around in the opposite direction

Tie off in the seam of the head/body join

Hide the end inside the body and cut off excess

Crochet Slang 101

Hot
Off
The
Hook

172

Joining Parts by Rooting

Throughout this book, you will be asked to insert your hook around the post of a finished part and crochet your stitches directly through the surface fabric. This is referred to as "rooting" the yarn, which is most commonly used to attach or "root" a doll's hair. This technique can also be used to place tails, ears, manes, etc.

With slip knot on the hook, insert hook under stitch post

Yarn over

Pull through loop

Yarn over

Complete the stitch

Crochet Slang 101

P roject

H alf

D one

173

About the Author (and The Floppies, too!)

Rachel Hilz
The Frog Hooker

Rachel Hilz, otherwise known as *The Frog Hooker* in the crochet community, is the creative mind behind *The Floppies* – a delightful collection of quirky amigurumi animal patterns featuring I-cord limbs. With a wild imagination and a passion for crafting, Rachel brings these adorable creatures to life with the swish of her wand... or hook. These Floppies are perfect for craft fairs, make wonderful gifts, and are loved by children (and the young at heart) everywhere!

Living on the picturesque Vancouver Island in British Columbia, Canada, Rachel is not just a *yarnie*, but also a dedicated military wife and the mum of two Autistic kids. This unique perspective enriches her work, as she understands the importance of creativity and play in nurturing young minds. Balancing chaos and creativity is always her baseline, and Rachel credits the Floppies for keeping her sane. Probably a little neurodivergent herself (or a lot, who's keeping track?), her designs encourage exploration of various crochet stitches and techniques, adding a playful twist to the traditional single crochet stitches that define most amigurumi. Each project is a fun and rewarding experience.

When not crocheting, Rachel enjoys writing children's books and spending time with her family and three small, somewhat yappy dogs. She can often be found on the beautiful hiking trails of the island, exploring lakes, forests, rivers, and the ocean. The photos of the Floppies featured in this book were taken while out on these hikes.

Join Rachel on a whimsical crochet journey as you create your very own Floppies, and be sure to hop into her Facebook group to share your creations at: https://www.facebook.com/groups/crochetcolony/

Website- www.froghookerdesigns.com
Facebook- www.facebook.com/froghooker
Instagram- @rachelshooksn'books
You Tube- https://www.youtube.com/FrogHooker

www.ingramcontent.com/pod-product-compliance
Lightning Source LLC
Chambersburg PA
CBHW041512120626
46551CB00018B/2397